**Michael Clark** is a lecturer in Graphic Design and a keen naturalist. He has illustrated *Badgers* by Ernest Neal and *Whales* by Nigel Bonner, exhibited drawings and paintings of mammals, and broadcast on the BBC radio programmes *Wildlife* and *The Living World*. He is a member of the Mammal Society and was a founder member of the British Deer Society.

'Excellent tips on everything from socks to frame of mind. Packed with personal experience, championing eyes and senses over technological ironmongery, it conveys the technique and excitement of observing animals and not merely ticking them off a list.'
*The Observer*

'Very, very practical . . . full of personal experiences and good ideas on how to do things. . . . A most useful and stimulating book.'
Dr Pat Morris on BBC Radio 4's *The Living World*

'Covers all the British groups, native and feral, from insectivores and rodents to carnivores and cetaceans, with advice on the individual methods of observing each.'
*The Times Educational Supplement*

'An indispensable mine of information . . . . Michael Clark has thought of and answered every question the beginner might ask, and has included so many tips on live trapping, photography and sound recording that the most experienced mammologist will find something new. . . . Excellent colour photographs, readable text.'
*Wildlife Review*

NATURE WATCH

# MAMMAL WATCHING

## Michael Clark

Hamlyn Paperbacks

To Molly Hopkyns and Dr John Hopkyns
*With affection and thanks for the countless hours
I have spent watching mammals on their land*

MAMMAL WATCHING
ISBN 0 600 20753 6

First published in Great Britain 1981
by Severn House Publishers Limited
Hamlyn Paperbacks edition 1983
Text © 1981 by Michael Clark
Drawings © 1981 by Severn House
Publishers Limited

Hamlyn Paperbacks are published by
The Hamlyn Publishing Group Ltd,
Astronaut House, Feltham,
Middlesex, England

Printed and bound in Great Britain by
Hazell Watson & Viney Limited, Aylesbury, Bucks

*Editorial:* Ian Jackson and Diana Levinson
*Design:* Michael Stannard

**Drawings by Michael Clark**

# Contents

Preface    6

Introduction    7

1   General thoughts and equipment    8

2   Hides, high seats and habitats    21

3   Small mammals    30
    Mole 38; shrews 39; voles 41; mice
    and rats 43; hedgehog 47

4   Bats    50

5   Gnawers and nibblers    69
    Rabbit 69; brown hare 73; mountain
    hare 75; red squirrel 76; grey
    squirrel 78; coypu 80

6   Grazers and browsers    81
    Red-necked wallaby 81; horses 82;
    deer 83: red 86, sika 91, fallow 92,
    roe 94, muntjac 95, Chinese water 106;
    reindeer 110; white cattle 110; feral
    goats and sheep 111

7   Predators    113
    Stoat and weasel 113; pine marten 115;
    polecat and ferret 116; fox 119;
    badger 123; otter and mink 129;
    wild cat 132

8   Marine mammals    134
    Whales 134; common and grey seal 139

9   Keeping the record straight    142

10   Moments of time    150

Appendices
    I Classification    164
    II Mammals and the law    167
    III Useful addresses    167

Further reading    170

Acknowledgements    173

Index    174

# Preface

Wherever you go in the world there are mammals to watch and each region has its particular points of interest. It is beyond the scope of this book to do more than mention in passing East Africa and the best places to watch such mammals as the great whales. So I have concentrated on Britain and much of what applies in this country can be said of watching in Europe. It is an amusing diversion to look at all the distribution maps in van den Brink's *A Field Guide to the Mammals of Britain and Europe* (1967) to see where the most species can be found in one area. Many ranges seem to overlap around the Spanish and French border in the Pyrenees.

In Europe the numbers of species increase to give variety to the types one can become familiar with at home. For example, a colleague of mine bird ringing in Switzerland caught a European free-tailed bat (*Tadarida teniotis*) in the Swiss Alps right in the north of its migration range. These bats (Molossidae) are quite unlike anything in Britain and it is well worth looking for chamois (*Rupicapra rupicapra*) and ibex (*Capra hircus*) or if you can use Longworth traps, catching the more varied small mammals. Garden dormice (*Eliomys quercinus*) are likely to turn up around houses and I have known of them entering holiday homes in southern France.

The mammals referred to in the text are all listed with their Latin names in Appendix I to save use of Latin throughout and all book references mentioned can be located in the Further reading section for full details.

# Introduction

When Ian Jackson of Severn House asked me to write this book I was delighted, but immediately concerned that the project would keep me indoors. However, the first draft was written in longhand on dog-eared sheets of notepaper under hedges, on cliffs, overlooking badger sets in woodland and under orchard apple trees.

As I have not had textbooks at hand I have made it very much a series of recalled incidents and opinions. The textbooks and field guides are widely available to refer to and I have tried to encourage watching rather than repeat published material. I have deliberately given extra attention to bat watching because this area is so neglected in existing literature and have used the little-documented muntjac deer as an example of how notes made from watching can be collated into useful graph form under subject headings.

I wanted to illustrate all parts of the book as fully as possible, particularly where points can be made that are not found in textbooks. One of the most useful of these books is the *Handbook of British Mammals* edited by Corbet and Southern (1977) and I make frequent references to this as the *Handbook*. The considerable gaps in my knowledge will be only too obvious.

I am deeply grateful for the great tolerance and help given by my wife Anna over the years of shared observation and I acknowledge the inspiration of all my associates who will probably recognise many of their views freely expressed here, particularly Dr Oliver Dansie, Clive Banks and Ralph Newton. My sheets of hardly legible manuscript were painstakingly typed out by Cathy Percival to whom I owe a great debt of thanks. Finally, my thanks to Ian Jackson and Diana Levinson for being such patient and helpful editors.

# 1 General thoughts and equipment

You can watch wild mammals almost anywhere from town and village to remote mountain or seashore. It is true that most mammals are active at dawn and dusk, but when we adapt our hours to theirs the rewards are great.

The theme of this book is the enjoyment of watching. The methods described provide a basis for all kinds of study. I have included drawing, photography and tape-recording, but the observer who simply sees and absorbs will always be the ultimate mammal watcher. Original observation cannot be replaced. Nor can you become a mammal watcher without becoming a watcher of birds, plants and insects too. You cannot, for example, study harvest mice without wanting to distinguish the grasses and sedges in which they live and construct their nests. That wasp nest dug out by the badgers you have been watching will interest you in itself. If the nest structure attracts you to Spradbery's book *Wasps* (1973) you will find a new world of interest.

We are fortunate in having superb field guides to our fauna and flora and no attempt has been made to include already published general identification material in this book. I have only added a number of illustrative points to hasten familiarity with the different species. These are based on gaps in the guides or particular aspects I have noticed along the way.

The first consideration is our approach to mammal watching. Our aim must be to disturb the animals we see as little as possible. I always remember a distant figure climbing over a footpath fence to enter an area of woods and fields where I was watching red deer feeding. I noticed the figure before he appeared because pigeons and small birds flew up and towards me – always a sign of approaching disturbance, usually by humans or dogs. The man was dressed in a brilliant fluorescent anorak and I was amazed to see him stop and raise binoculars to a flock of finches flying away on one side of the path. It is true that fluorescent weatherproof clothing is essential for hill walking and climbing where the need to be located by rescuers is always a possibility, but for watching wildlife one should stick to drab, camouflaged clothing and when necessary resort to face camouflage, too. I watched the man go on his way with fleeing birds disappearing before him and could only think that he was probably good at tail markings.

Basic stalking technique is a fundamental skill. Walk through a

Figure 1 Wild mammals quickly notice light features; if you look at these photographs with half-closed eyes, the advantages of camouflage will be obvious.

habitat as slowly as you can and then halve the speed: we all move too quickly even after years of experience. Successful watching depends so much upon your state of mind and temperament. If you are going out after a tense day or have had problems getting to a site, all the anxiety goes with you and can ruin the one part of the day which could have been a success. You conclude that it was 'one of those days', but the visit may have been different. Stop and relax, even if you have arrived late. Start watching, whether this means stalking quietly or sitting waiting, in a fresh frame of mind. You cannot 'forget your troubles', but when you relax for the first time in hours you can gain a new outlook on all kinds of subjects.

Modern society has largely eliminated quietness and contemplation. These may be a by-product of mammal watching, but you will find them valuable nevertheless. There are many things which contribute to a hobby or interest and I have often wondered how much these aspects attract me out of doors. In particular, as winter ends and evenings lengthen, the urge to be out and away from the constraints of work and routine are powerful. The lure of wilderness and countryside becomes very intense to the addict.

Books by the old village poachers often capture this need. It is as if the taking of game is only part of the story; the real attraction is being out-doors in the countryside when most people are a-bed. Their poverty and the excitement of evading capture add spice, but at the root of it is a love of the woods and fields. James Hawker in *A Victorian Poacher: James Hawker's Journal* noted: 'I have spent hours in that lane sitting like a cat. The more quiet you sit, the better the chance of getting game'. This is the clue to the best results, in any habitat. It is the hours you put in and the way you behave whilst there. The cats are perhaps the finest mammal watchers in the animal kingdom. The bigger the area, the greater the temptation to keep on walking and hoping, although a good site may necessitate a very long walk. This is particularly true of mountainous areas, but it is how you react when you get there that is crucial.

I have visited a very small wood, just under two acres in size, almost daily for ten years. Within this small area I have enjoyed more hours of actual mammal watching per visit than at any other of the countless sites I have visited. It is how well you get to know an area rather than its size which is important.

We will consider mammals in all kinds of localities, but I am not writing for the tick hunter: one who ticks off each species as it is seen or photo-graphed. Nor is this book about only the rarer species or about rushing to see an unusual vagrant. The long-established watcher who concen-trates on pine martens, for example, will be beyond the basic principles outlined here.

Your ability to be calm and relaxed when watching depends a great deal on the comfort of your clothing. Mammal watching is usually done when temperatures are low and even if your walk to a site on a hot summer evening is sticky, you soon cool down and the warm clothing can seem inadequate within half an hour.

The first priority is a warm, rainproof jacket. These are available in many different styles and at a variety of prices. Go for the most expensive you can afford in a drab dark green or brown. One range has an expensive zip and popper jacket with warm lining. It includes a detachable hood and can be re-proofed easily. The various types are listed in Appendix III and you will find that most fishermen and naturalists end up with this kind of oiled jacket. They protect the body very well and include a useful game pocket inside. After you have rolled through a few hedges and crawled along a ditch or two, your jacket will soon be acceptable to deer and foxes.

Footwear is important and different habitats call for different types of boot. Wellingtons are invaluable in all kinds of localities and drab green is ideal. I once asked at a Game Fair why one famous company puts a bright red-and-white logo on the front of their green boots when the idea is to camouflage the wearer from game. Nobody seemed to know. I wear moleskin plus-four trousers with them because they are loose at the calf and cover the outside top of the boot. With more shaping than most these boots really are more comfortable over distances than cheaper wellingtons. Do not try to wear flared jeans, for example, inside them; long socks and plus-fours are best and if these do not flop over the label you can subdue the bright corporate symbol with a splash of drab paint.

In many conditions, and especially when a lot of walking is involved, hill boots are much more suitable. The type of shop which allows you to try on a wide range of boots with a heavy sock is best for your purchase. Keep a thin pair of socks on underneath and fit both feet. In use, always wear a light pair of tennis or similar socks underneath and thick climbing socks on top. This will keep the socks from slipping under the heel and reduce the risk of blisters. Never tie laces round the heel which encourages blisters and keep the boots well proofed with waterproof polish. Laces last longer if you rub wet-proof types of polish into them during polishing sessions. Unless you want to climb as well and prefer a stiff boot for narrow toe holds, keep to supple soles.

Long socks usually shrink and wear out quickly, but I have found that the thermal types are not only warm, but outlast the usual climbing or gamekeeper-type socks. Combined with cotton undersocks, plus-fours and canvas gaiters for rough bracken or gorse country, you will enjoy long walks and wildlife watching in comfort. If you are liable to blister at the heel, put plasters on before you even start new ones. Carry plasters in a flat tin in your top pocket and stop at once should blisters develop. If you persist you may be in acute discomfort and this may prevent you from subsequent walks over the days which follow.

You can buy a hat and gloves to blend with cover. These are readily available in surplus stores and a peak on the hat helps when viewing wildlife into a bright sky with dark ground. Pulled down, it concentrates the area of vision (through binoculars too, if necessary) onto the dark area. With the confusion of the contrasting areas gone, the eyes see into the poorly lit scenery with greater clarity. Drab green mittens provide the ideal combination of warmth, camouflage and retained dexterity for binoculars or camera. Gloves tend to be too warm for much of the year and clumsy in general use. Hands show up so clearly that mittens are helpful even in warm weather. They are cooler than gloves and seem to allow the fingers to adjust to surrounding temperatures without discomfort.

Face masks can be purchased from sports shops or surplus stores. They are used by pigeon shooters and range from a net which covers the head completely, apart from an eye slit, to face netting that straps round head and neck with elastic. I have used both over the years and find them very useful at times. They tend to irritate the eyes and mouth, but if kept in a pocket and only used when a particular need arises, are bearable when you are stationary. Some mammals are extremely shy and individuals within a species can vary from very bold to highly nervous. At some badger sets, for example, the animals may tolerate virtually any clothing, but at others a face mask improves chances of nervous individuals approaching and behaving normally. Exceptions can occur however: I was once asked to take a press photographer to a set to photograph the badgers to promote the work of the local trust for nature conservation. To my horror he arrived straight from a fashion show with appropriate bright blue ski jacket and matching accessories. We sat under a holly bush, somewhat apart, and I had to whisper to him in the dark later that the badgers were out. In spite of this he obtained the best photograph of a pair of badgers I have seen at this set. I have an idea that they just could not believe it and had stood transfixed by his appearance at that moment.

The need to keep warm is essential on draughty earth banks, in high seats and amongst damp vegetation. I often wonder how much I have increased my chances of aches and pains in later years from staying out at all hours in damp, cold habitats. Small inflatable cushions (mostly used by fishermen) can be purchased and easily carried folded in a pocket or bag. The double-seated moleskin type of plus-four insulates well and thermal 'long john' underwear with deep back vest really helps maintain body heat. With similar types of socks, you can then forget the temperature and concentrate on your interests. All this clothing is expensive initially, but I have found that it lasts and outlives cheaper alternatives and is more economical in the long run.

Insects can be a major form of irritation and the net face masks can help. There are special scentless repellents sold at high prices, but the cheapest chain store chemist gels or liquids are just as good. Early insect repellents were both very unpleasant and obvious to wild mammals when the watcher was seated for an hour or so near earths or paths. I recall two novice watchers who arrived to be shown where to watch the badgers, reeking of the most incredible repellent. It kept me at bay and they returned to say no badgers had turned up.

Beekeepers' net headgear is very effective against mosquitos although midges can creep through. You can use the same hat with a finer net but this darkens everything and you may want to spray light areas black with paint. You can look very silly sitting with this headgear on at dusk without a bee in sight, but never let such considerations put you off. In parts of Scotland, Alaska and other northern countries it is no exaggeration to say that a beekeeper's hat is ideal headgear on the hills in summer.

If I had to choose only one piece of optical equipment to spend the rest of my life with, I would go for my binoculars. Once you have selected a pair, they should go everywhere with you. Never leave them at home. It is always that day you will need them most and a valuable identification may be lost through lack of detail. The advantage of the smaller glasses is that they can be slipped into a gadget bag with photographic materials. Equipment left at home is a waste of capital outlay, too.

Care must be taken in the way you handle field glasses. Always put the strap round your neck before use. This may seem obvious, but people often do not bother especially when lending the glasses to someone else. One hard knock can be very expensive and inconvenient to put right. Once prisms are jarred out of alignment, you must get them repaired by professionals; never work on them yourself. It is also worthwhile to check your focus on arrival at a site. Set the glasses on middle distance making sure that both eyepieces are in focus. There are few things more frustrating than hurriedly looking at a distant animal and finding the binoculars are set close-up.

I strongly advocate the small, light binoculars because the larger, heavy types can strain your neck or shoulders after a long walk. They may be optically excellent but that dull ache at the back of the neck can spoil a day out. Good light gathering power is another priority. If you combine the use of a telescope with the binoculars you may want lower magnifications for the latter, but I prefer a large image size of × 10. Small glasses can be held still and pick up the mammal without difficulty as you raise the glasses and temporarily lose visual contact. This is the time when glasses of very high magnification can be a disaster. You cannot easily connect with the animal in view during the 'blind time' as the binoculars meet your eyes. I would not go above × 10 for this reason.

Ideally you should divide the magnification (first figure) into light gathering (second figure) and have a figure of between about 4 and 8. I managed for years with a very good quality 6 × 30 pair of light binoculars and now have more magnification and brighter image quality in a small pair of 10 × 40s. 9 × 56 or 10 × 70 may seem very desirable for night use when badger or fox watching, for example, but you lose your ability to see well at night increasingly after adolescence and a factor of × 70 may be wasted after your mid-twenties.

Never buy binoculars without first trying many types to see which suits you best. Take your time and aim for the 7 × 50 to 10 × 50 range. These will be excellent for mammal and birdwatching. A recent survey by the Royal Society for the Protection of Birds showed that birdwatchers prefer × 10 magnification and I have not found bat watching any more difficult at this magnification. There is a traditional prejudice against × 10 because of hand shake, but once you have tried the newer compact types with their bright image quality you will see how easy they are to hold still. If you have not changed your binoculars for years, I strongly recommend investigation of the recent types.

Specialist types of binoculars and telescopes include the range of image intensifiers and infra-red makes. These are available increasingly for non-military use, but are still very costly. I illustrated the infra-red binoculars used in Dr Christopher Cheeseman's badger research for the Ministry of Agriculture, Fisheries and Food. These drawings were used for Dr Ernest Neal's book on this species (see Further reading). A very powerful lamp is located above the binoculars which works from a battery pack carried from a shoulder sling. All except infra-red light is filtered off and the binoculars show the illuminated scene as a pale green. You can there-fore see clearly to the extent of the lamplight. Modern developments in powerful 'lamping' torches (for night shooting) combined with binoculars can achieve a similar effect, but the animals are always aware

Figure 2 Dr Christopher Cheeseman watching badgers at night with infra-red binoculars.

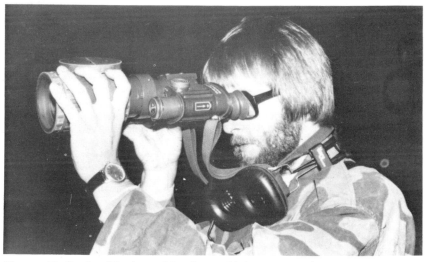

Figure 3 Dr Stephen Harris watching foxes with image intensifier binoculars.

of the unfiltered light (see Appendix III). Such are the rapid changes in technology that within a year of doing the drawings, the infra-red binoculars were superseded by image intensifiers which magnify available light greatly without the use of a lamp and are therefore less cumbersome. Both types are now in use and reveal the world at night very successfully, but the prices are too high for the amateur as yet.

With Dr Stephen Harris in Bristol and Dr Cheeseman in Gloucester-shire, I have watched badgers, followed them back to sets after they have fed and then, thanks to the radio tracking equipment, stood right over the parts of tunnels where the badgers were resting underground. All on very dark nights.

Telescopes can be difficult to use initially, but with experience, many watchers find them indispensable, especially on the open hill or on the coast. A colleague likes to use 7 × 50 binoculars for his general watching and on location of animals, turns to his up to × 60 telescope. For red deer on open moorland and otters, seals or dolphins on coastal sites in good light conditions they are excellent. (Whatever your specialist interest, you should never ignore the waders and ducks at such places. One of the compensations for hours of waiting for certain mammals is the bird life and, indeed, flora, insect life and landscape.)

Armed with your aid or aids to watching, your dull coat, ('camouflage' jackets usually stand out much too strongly) and warm underwear, successful watching should come your way. It is, however, still essential to stalk carefully and sit still. If you stick to eight or nine slow paces, stand and survey, more slow paces, stand and survey and so on, you have the best chance of seeing wildlife before it sees you. Always think of yourself as an intruder in that habitat, especially in the last stages of approach to

Figure 4 Walk as slowly as possible when you are stalking and raise your binoculars inconspicuously.

animals you have observed. Check the wind direction and always try to walk with the breeze into your face. A small linen bag with chalk dust can help show an indistinct wind direction. Crumbled up dry leaves will do, or a handkerchief held square to the breeze to detect the movement. Some watchers prefer to use their binoculars only when they have

Figure 6 A wood mouse near a bait site amongst woodland leaf litter, branches and dog's mercury.

spotted an animal but I like to 'sweep' cover with them. It helps to slow you down, even if as a general rule you can locate animals unaided at first. In some circumstances it is possible to walk with binoculars held to your eyes. This is awkward, but if animals are in view, it stops you having to raise and lower the glasses repeatedly on approach.

Crawling, lying prone and edging forward or freezing for several minutes are all part of the good watcher's repertoire. There are exceptions however and, as mentioned in Chapter 6 a noisy, open approach to deer for example can work in areas where they are used to the general public.

Figure 5 Test wind direction when approaching mammals and avoid skylines.

This locates herds or individuals and as long as you keep walking past and then return with a very stealthy, down-wind approach out of sight all should go well.

When you hear a twig crack or a sudden movement in cover nearby, do not react immediately. Train yourself not to crane your neck hurriedly or peer round with abrupt movements. If anything is going to appear, it is likely to reveal itself before long. The very fact that it has been noisy indicates that the animal is unaware of you, but your advantage is easily lost by over-reaction. On the other hand, your scent may have strayed round to an unnoticed animal and the sound may indicate that it is startled. It may tolerate this unless your movement confirms danger. Curiosity can turn to alarm when you are watching one mammal and another is at hand that you have not seen. Always be prepared for an undetected individual or even several to be present and act accordingly.

Avoid skylines because a silhouette is easily picked out, especially if it

Figure 7 A young dormouse next to a typical summer breeding nest in brambles.

Figure 8 An opened harvest mouse nest, one metre above ground in tall grasses next to a wheat field.

is moving. You will notice how a figure shows up outside a fir plantation as it crosses vertical black trunk after trunk in the comparative light. What a contrast it is to peer into firs and try to see a figure amongst the dark trees.

Be aware that when you enter habitats you are starting off with many disadvantages compared with the animals which live there so try to picture yourself at a distance in each setting you come to. Step outside yourself, as it were, to see what impression you are making. Be very self-critical and merge in with the countryside around you.

The past discussion largely implies watching alone and you are invariably more successful when by yourself. Mammal watching is,

Figure 10 A figure against the light is very obvious so try to keep a low profile as necessary.

perhaps, the activity of the loner. You may feel that all pleasures are better shared but the problem is that when you add another person, you probably halve your success rate. This varies from species to species, it is true, but as a general rule, your success rate will decline in inverse proportion to the number of people in a group.

I always remember seeing my first fox cubs as a lad. I was able to crawl right up to the earth and the cubs were almost playing on my feet as I sat by the entrance. They were at the age of relative trust and innocence. In great anticipation I took my parents down the following night and despite a long wait we saw nothing apart from mosquitos and the odd rabbit. I realised later that the vixen would have scented me and had probably moved the cubs, but I have been shy of taking people in groups to watch ever since. We make so much noise when in a group and people tend to whisper. Four or eight footfalls make much more noise than the lone, careful walker's step and several human scents increase the risk of detection.

Figure 9 A hedgehog's winter nest opened to show the occupant. A favourite hibernation site is under compost in neglected corners of gardens.

One final point to remember when going out to watch: record your observations with as much detail and accuracy as you can. Inaccurate, partially recalled data is worthless and can be positively damaging if it is used in evidence for something connected with wild animal behaviour. I deal with recording systems in the final chapter, but at the first, original stage detail is essential. Ideally carry a notebook and pencil or pen with you. A note on the spot is worth many recalled observations. I have found it possible to write as I watch badgers, for example, at a set, as things actually happen. An accurate watch is essential and you can add details of weather conditions, temperature and times as you go along. It is best to write on your knee underneath your coat where there is no danger of the movements and light paper showing up. When you get home you will find the writing very distorted because you were looking elsewhere, but it is surprising how well we can write out of view of our eyes. Copy up notes into a bound diary (see Chapter 9).

Do notes, illustrations and the grid references as soon as possible at home. I keep a daily diary which is largely on natural history themes and includes glued-in cuttings. You should add grid references from a map and additional names if you do not already know the area well. It is all a matter of habit. If you note down everything you see, say for example, the time, weather conditions and locality where a badger crossed the road in front of you, you will build up a collection of sightings that take on increasing significance as time goes on. Behaviour and habits only fall into a pattern when you have written material to compare over long periods of time.

One of my particular interests is muntjac deer behaviour. In conjunction with Dr Oliver Dansie, I have noted down records of the birth of fawns, barking, antler drop and other activities over the years. Only now, as I extract this information from the diaries, can I see the patterns of behaviour emerge. You find fawns born in each month, adults barking regularly and variations in loss of antlers. The watcher must inevitably become the writer and recorder. You cannot watch in a vacuum without wanting to express the pleasure of that watching – through notes, drawings, photographs and even tape-recordings.

As well as your notebook, a tape measure, × 10 hand lens, plastic bags, penknife and string are useful as aids to accurate recording and for carrying home material. But watching is the most important basis for recording and, as I will say again and again, there are dangers of becoming overloaded with equipment. Binoculars and a reliable watch with a scrap of paper and pencil are really the only necessary aids to general study. Map and compass are essential in remote or hill country, but travel light. You will enjoy watching all the more.

# 2 Hides, high seats and habitats

The well-prepared observer will enjoy exploring and watching much more than the casual visitor to a site. Most types of mammal watching do not require the use of hides but they are necessary when a particular habitat in the countryside has an enduring attraction of some kind. Hides can retain scent and warn mammals of human presence, but when combined with high seats can be very popular with the public. A well-known example is Grizedale in the Midlands of England where the Forestry Commission have encouraged the observation of wildlife, particularly deer, in their natural setting. They have a Wildlife Centre there which is now a feature of many other areas of outstanding countryside.

Mammals may be tied to certain sites such as water holes in Africa or their breeding nests or earths. Generally, however, away from carefully managed sites, a hide is not appropriate and can simply draw unwelcome attention to a particular place. We are a destructive race and a hide left in the countryside can be an easy target. Badger sets are an obvious place for a secure watching screen, but these have severe limitations even on private land and I have reservations about erecting what can amount to sheds next to badger sets. Badgers usually dismantle 'natural' hides of bracken and branches if they get used to the human scent concentrated in such sites, whereas high seats (enclosed or open seating on top of some kind of ladder made of metal or wood) are a much more sensible proposition. They are widely used in deer stalking and in watching areas such as Cannock Chase, Thetford and the New Forest. They seem to be far less obtrusive than hides and merge with tree foliage above ground level in summer. I have used a hide in a private orchard and obtained a sequence of photographs of wild deer, but by far the most successful watching I have done has been from a metal high seat on an adjoining nature reserve. A simple screening of wood round the top gives shelter and obscures the human silhouette. From this raised position I have watched bats, mice, rabbits, badgers, foxes, deer, stoats and birds regularly. The most important factor is that a raised position sends your scent over the heads of the mammals below. We risk detection by mammals as soon as our scent drifts towards them and a hide on the ground so often seems to be fixed in the wrong position. This limitation is not so important in a high seat because the scent drifts gently upwards even if the wind is behind you.

Cars can also be used as hides and safari tours of East Africa are largely based on this form of mobile hide. Mammals will react if a figure gets out of a vehicle, but are very tolerant otherwise. One of our local muntjac illustrated the way in which wild deer which have experienced frighteningly close contact with Man can, despite this, be indifferent to vehicles. One day I had driven out of our gate with the family and saw the green-collared doe muntjac whose recorded sightings we log, crossing the village green towards the road. I stopped and despite a car full of humans peering out at her, she walked across in front of us, up into the hedge and away. If I had got out of the car she would have panicked and fled back across the green.

Deer in deer parks can be approached in cars although again they will panic if you suddenly appear from inside. I had a memorable 'stag night', as it were, when tape-recording two fighting red deer. I heard their clash of antlers when recording roaring and drove to within fifty metres. I

Figure 11 Canvas hides are useful and can be moved easily, but, unlike high seats, they may concentrate human scent.

leant across, opened the passenger door and put a microphone parabola on the ground. The fight was spectacular and a low fence by the estate road was smashed as the antlers met. They fought through a bush as if it were not there and broke off for long enough to strut along the remaining pieces of fence and crash in on each other again. As the antlers meet in their complex of tines such contests are a test of strength rather than a fight to the death. The power of fighting deer is incredible to experience at close quarters and to my delight the stags came closer and closer. They then broke off and strutted, roaring at each other to stand either side of the open car door. I was suddenly aware that they might treat the car door with the same disdain they had for the fence and the bush. If they had gone for each other at that point I am sure they would have removed the door. I also had the uneasy feeling that they might want to come and sit inside with me. It was one of the most exciting moments of mammal watching I have experienced. With the smell of rutting stags and their roaring ringing in my ears I felt a part of the deer herd myself.

The stags paused, strutted off and their antlers then met again with almost an explosion. They finally went struggling down the hill into the darkness and one broke away running off with the victor in pursuit. The car can then be the best and safest hide in some circumstances. A boat can also enable close approach to mammals and I have watched seals from boats on the east coast where they are quite used to passing craft (see Chapter 8).

If you have a site where a hide might be useful, you can either make your own or purchase one. The purchased hides are made of fairly thin material and should not be left out beyond the time you intend to use them. I left one out during an autumn but found it collapsed and starting to rot in a few weeks. It was rather annoying to find brown rats living underneath the crumpled hide. Perhaps they were watching me. If you have access to old, drab green tarpaulin or heavy-duty canvas, you can make your own hide with stakes and twine. A simple, single-sided screen

Figure 12 Single screens are adequate for watching certain mammals such as water voles.

is often enough for mammal watching, or a two-sided one, set at right angles with viewing holes cut. Synthetic hessian, tan coloured polypropylene in 94 × 59 centimetre tapes, is very light and will stand a good deal of punishment from the weather (see Appendix III). Natural hides can be unobtrusive constructions of layered branches and available bracken, gorse or leaves. You may need several around a site because of the problem of wind direction. I used bracken at a set once, but the badgers kept dragging away the pieces I had gathered and taking them down as welcome bedding. Vandals finished the job and I realised how unfortunate attention can be drawn to a set by constructions of this kind. Think hard before you decide to build or buy a hide. If it is appropriate on undisturbed private property by all means have a try. I would not advise the purchase of a hide until you have tried one out as they can limit your vision, trap human scent and become very cramped.

The bird hide technique of two people going to the hide and then one walking away is not necessary for mammal watching. You should however, leave the hide carefully if the mammals have appeared and are now active round about. The birdwatcher or photographer waits for the return of a colleague so that the birds are not aware that someone has been staying by their nest. Mammals soon become accustomed to a hide and accept it as a safe part of their environment. You can edge a hide closer to a water vole run, for example, but it is less vital to move it as gradually as at a bird nest.

You may purchase the Arley type of high seat (see Appendix III) or build your own, but with both you must observe the highest standards of safety. Even the manufactured types can be dangerous if sited badly on uneven ground and it is best to rope or chain them to a tree. Always climb into them from the inside, never from the front or outside which may topple the framework over. It is straightforward to make up your own high seat with a ladder leading up into tree branches which can be adapted for comfortable sitting.

Most of us become interested in watching wildlife through access to countryside of one kind or another. How much you see depends greatly upon where you live and the chances you have to watch elsewhere, at home and abroad. Clearly, some habitats are more interesting than

Figure 13 High seats can be either a simple ladder combined with a secure wooden platform (left) or an all metal construction incorporating a ladder as in the two-man Arley (right).

others for various reasons, including lack of human disturbance. You must not be discouraged if you visit a wood for the first time and after two hours do not even see a mammal. If I visit a new site, I may walk around for a long time first looking at the field signs: footprints, paths off rides, droppings, earths and scents. Skill in reading these signs can be developed wherever you are, and the paths used habitually by mammals will be one of the first things you encounter. Such signs include hairs left on barbed wire, scent and tracks in sand, mud or snow. I followed a badger's tracks for over a mile last winter and discovered a new set of earths to watch at. Be careful with the identification of tracks, droppings and signs of eating because some are very variable and mistakes can easily be made. Use them in conjunction with other observations. Mammals do leave signs everywhere, however, such as foxes leaving food débris round their earths; rabbits damaging trees; deer fraying stems and branches; vole and mouse feeding and nesting signs; even otters sliding in mud down banks. An analysis of the owl pellets you can find in a habitat will tell you much about the small mammals present. Good guides

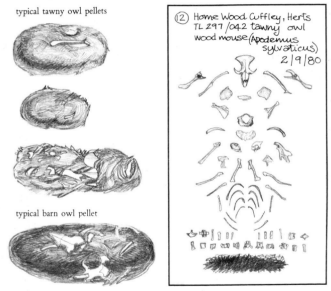

typical tawny owl pellets

typical barn owl pellet

⑫ Home Wood Cuffley, Herts TL 297/042 tawny owl wood mouse (Apodemus sylvaticus) 2/9/80

Figure 14 Owl pellets are a good guide to small mammal species to be found in a locality. Novices can display the bone remains as shown and learn to identify the different skulls with the help of a field guide.

such as Bang and Dahlstrom's *Animal tracks and signs* and D. W. Yalden's Mammal Society booklet (see Further reading) are available and the analysis is a study in itself.

Field craft should develop with your watching skills. Recently three friends and I were walking along the woodland edge of an estate looking at fox runs and earths. At one point we caught the fresh scent of fox and a metre or so on spotted the animal on the edge of a hedgerow, closely watching two rabbits. We literally looked over the fox's ears at the rabbits: the wind was blowing into our faces and the fox did not stop staring ahead, absolutely still. Then the fox made its move, rushing unsuccessfully at the nearest rabbit. The rabbit vanished into a warren in the hedge and the fox trotted on across the field.

You might have to be content with several blank visits but the field signs will give you many clues as to what you can expect to see by patient watching in the future. The time of day is important, as we will see later, but daytime visits can be useful for sweeping paths and preparing viewing sites round badger sets for example. A swept path made by taking a broom and clearing the broken twigs and litter from woodland walks so that stalking can be silent can be surprisingly helpful in places.

Approaches to landowners and farmers are always best if made in person and it may be obvious, but do avoid mealtimes. A telephone call to ask for a convenient time may be all that is needed to find out if an area of countryside can be visited. Always explain your interest and keep your kind hosts informed of all the things you see. You can have an important function as a warden of the land when you come across interlopers. Direct trespassers to the nearest route off the land or, if you actually come across unlawful digging at badger sets for example, go and call the police at once. Respect the property as if it were your own. When mammal watching you will soon find that certain types of mammals are very common in some habitats and much rarer in others. One of the

Figure 15 If you have regular access to woodland for mammal watching, swept paths can be very helpful for silent stalking. Oddly enough, the wild mammals seem to follow them more, despite the human scent.

most dramatic examples of this is in bat numbers over wooded lakes when compared with those in fir plantations. If you watch bats by an old-established pond amongst dense, old deciduous trees you may see dozens of them in flight at dusk on a warm night. In the same weather conditions, if you walk round a dense fir plantation which covers many hundreds of acres and has no standing water, you will probably only see two or three rapidly flying bats looking as if they are going somewhere fast. Obviously some rare species will be found only in local parts of the country and in certain types of terrain, such as chamois in the Alps, but we can make some generalisations about different habitats and the mammals you are likely to find there.

**Gardens** A variety of small mammals occur depending upon cover and the tolerance of owners. Gardens can be adapted to encourage mammals by the erection of a mammal table and a hedgehog nest-box (see Chapter 3). Bats in house roofs or bat boxes produce numbers feeding over gardens. Gardens may be visited by foxes and in places, deer and badgers too. Sometimes these species are resident without the owner's knowledge.

**Parks, open spaces and golf courses** Small mammals, hedgehogs and bats in good numbers especially if there are lakes or ponds. Rabbits, hares, stoats and weasels, foxes and sometimes badgers and deer also occur. The amount of cover in the way of hedgerows, scrub and copse and the general management will influence the numbers of animals present.

**Open farmland and estates** A mixture of small wooded areas and open fields with mixed arable and dairy farming will give a rich variety

Figure 16 Wetland flora between cultivated farmland forms precious wilderness areas for wildlife. A search here revealed the old breeding nest of a harvest mouse in cocksfoot grass against thorn scrub (see figure 17) and the occupied nest shown in figure 8.

Figure 17 A harvest mouse nest site in a habitat generally good for small mammals. Where grasses and scrub give ground cover next to reed beds by a stream, the mice have a relatively secure site. The old nest is at the centre bottom of the picture in the grass. As the wheat matured next to this area, the mice colonised the crop too.

of habitats for wild mammals. Small mammals including, locally, dormice and harvest mice, hedgehogs, rabbits, hares and the predators (badger, fox, stoat and weasel), fallow, roe and muntjac deer depending on locality. Copses around old pits are valuable centres of activity and farm or village ponds will have a variety of bats.

**Old deciduous woodland** All types of mammal will be found in this habitat but the main centres of activity will be on the borders. It provides cover for foxes, badgers and deer which feed out into surrounding open areas. Dormice may occur together with the less common bat species.

**Fir plantations** These will have an abundance of small mammals in the early stages of growth and deer later on as the plantations thicken up with ground cover. In maturity bats will not frequent them in large numbers unless roosts are available and the small mammals survive more on the path edges, but deer continue to retreat into the dark cover afforded. Feeding out is at dawn and dusk. Foxes are common as are polecats in certain places and badgers.

**Old pits, gravel workings and refuse tips** Rabbits proliferate in pit edges; foxes and badgers like the easy digging on bank sides. At refuse tips rats are abundant and bats feed overhead, especially noctules.

Figure 18 Intensive farming leaves fewer and fewer uncultivated areas for wildlife and neglected pits such as this may become ideal sites for watching rabbits, stoats, weasels, foxes and badgers.

**Wetland, marshes, ponds and lakes** Harvest mice, water shrews and water voles occur here and they are often good sites to watch stoats and weasels hunting, as well as being ideal bat sites. Coypu are found in East Anglia; mink in many localities and otters in some.

**Rivers, estuaries and the coast** These provide an extension of the marshland and lake habitats with chances of seeing otters, seals, dolphins and porpoises. At sea whales can be seen especially from ships and boats chartered on known migration routes.

**Moorland and mountain** Small mammals survive in surprisingly high altitudes; foxes, pine martens and polecats occur in places as do wild cats, red deer, goats and ponies.

A very good guide to habitats and the typical animals of the major regions on a worldwide basis is *The Living World of Animals* which is set out almost entirely on an ecological basis (see Further reading).

# 3 Small mammals

The best way to watch the small mammals in a garden is to construct a cat-proof free-range enclosure adjoining the house around a window which, ideally, can be opened for direct access onto a small feeding area. The same principles then apply as for feeding birds at your bird-table: daily food must be put out suitable for the species present. There should be rough ground and ample grass cover around the enclosure to give the small mammals safe access in and out at ground level. There is no need to introduce captured mammals because the wild species quickly discover that there is a safe area with regular food available. The exit and entry gaps in the wire at the sides can be subterranean and a small platform on which the food is placed in front of the window creates a focal point for the small mammal activity. Mine has a back window overlooking a steep bank and I have found bank voles, field voles, wood mice, yellow-necked mice and even house mice which are normally shy when outdoors, coming to feed. At night the light from the house gives illumination although when accustomed to the enclosure all these species also come out in daylight.

Figure 19 Enclosed small mammal feeding areas attract a variety of species depending on the food put out and the cover in the garden. Access is at the base of the frame under grass. The netting must not be more than one centimetre square or birds will get in.

Bank voles are the most entertaining and confident visitors in daytime. My visiting yellow-necked mice got too fat to use the exits easily, but it is best not to enlarge the routes too much or rats may be attracted. Much as I enjoy rat watching, an area of rough cover is bad enough for the enthusiastic gardeners in the family and a thriving rat colony can push tolerance a little too far. My enclosure has been used for edible dormice (the most unfriendly small mammals I have come across with a bite to match that of a polecat), ferrets and polecats. The window access to the enclosure makes watching very easy and photography more feasible.

The mammal watching enclosure is more expensive than a bird-table, but it makes regular watching of wild small mammals possible virtually round the clock. We have many shrews in the garden, but I had never previously been able to see them. They do not seem to bait well, although, admittedly, suitable food was rarely put out for them. Away from gardens, baiting with rolled oats or mixed corn and artificial covers such as corrugated iron sheets on grass can give good views of small mammals. The problem with baiting is that feeding sites tend simply to be areas where you can see mammals running out to retrieve food for storage. This is fine for photography and the mammals will linger as their confidence grows, but you do not really get acquainted with their behaviour. Uncovering a sheet of corrugated metal used as artificial cover in grassland may show you the voles underneath, but they quickly scatter and are very nervous when they return (see page 41).

Small mammal watching has provided me with many exciting baiting site observations as well as regular views when watching badgers and surprise incidents. On one occasion a wood mouse appeared at the side of my head, climbing through a hawthorn about a metre up in the branches as I sat deer watching at dawn. It clambered about with great agility and seemed to make for rose hips growing into the thorns on one side. Another wood mouse climbed a narrow hornbeam to lose itself amongst foliage about six metres up.

However, to watch and really get to know individual small mammals the captive colony is invaluable and my most enjoyable hours of this kind of mammal watching were spent in my teens when I kept a colony of wood mice. I constructed as complicated a home for them as possible, full of tunnels and nest-boxes and as long as there was a grip they could run up nearly vertical linking tunnels. The main focus of the complex consisted of two large, dry aquariums and two deep boxes. All tunnels between these had glass tops and because all the parts were arranged in stages at different levels, all parts except the nest-boxes inside were visible. At first, I used a dull red light at night as the wood mice were conveniently active when I was home in the evenings and when going to bed. I then found that normal electric light was perfectly acceptable to them.

Ventilation and ample dry bedding are essential to all captive mammals. As much variation in food as possible should be encouraged: to a staple diet of oats, grass and water daily you can add such items as peanuts,

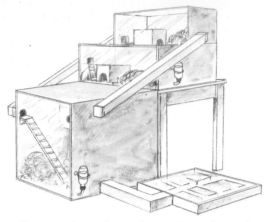

Figure 20 A small mammal complex used to study a colony of wood mice. Access to all parts of the system is essential.

hamster mixture food from pet shops, sunflower seeds, biscuit, apple, pear, tomato, cucumber, parsley, cabbage, spinach, ant eggs and all kinds of insects. Tinned dog food may be added, but clean out the enclosure carefully every day if it is used.

The lives of mice consist of a basic routine of eating, sleeping, courting, breeding, nest-building and food storage. They constantly move their bedding and food stores, explore their territory and sort out their social orders for which scenting is very important. Nest construction and food storage is very actively practised. One evening I noted the distance travelled by a mouse after I had filled one of the food trays. It ran from the tray, down a wooden path, dropped a seed into its box, rushed back and repeated the process. In twenty minutes I watched the mouse run the equivalent of over 300 metres and I fell asleep to the sound of it still running up and down. Similarly a yellow-necked mouse I marked with a tiny patch of nail varnish kept returning to one of my live traps in our loft, a distance of up to 500 m. After that it either gave up (having done 50 m, 100 m, 200 m and finally 500 m trips in one week) or was caught by a predator as it grumbled on its way to the 'dining room' again.

One observation I vividly recall from the hours of absorbed watching was when a mouse worked out an easier way to collect its food store. It had been running from the food tray down a run to the nest-box below and then it stopped apparently noticing that the seeds had fallen from the upper floor to just outside the nest-box. It started to push and drop seeds from its mouth over the edge and once a heap had formed, it went down and stored these using a much simpler and shorter trip in and out of the box from just outside it. I would not have believed a mouse could think things out so clearly if I had not watched it happen before my very eyes.

The courtship of captive mice is a mixture of chasing and fighting, and the reactions of ears, raised hairs and body attitudes are fascinating to watch. Females often stop running if the males lose interest and run back to encourage them, only to rush off again when they follow – the old 'stop it, I like it' routine. Washing is both a displacement activity when the mice are frightened and a genuine matter of personal hygiene.

Two female mice often seemed to look after one family: the actual mother and a sibling from one of her earlier litters, the younger one being allowed to collect up young if scattered from the mother during disturbance. You can see how the young develop and explore, and compare litter sizes between different females in the same colony when they first become independent. Old females which became particularly irritable when pregnant dominated the colony, which settled down to a maximum of fifteen mice. Overcrowding always produces aggression, failed litters and cannibalism. I finally released the colony after a year with a large store of food in the same area of woodland in which I had originally caught the nucleus.

The wood mice were much more interesting than all the other types of mice and voles which I have kept. Harvest mice come a close second and have enjoyed a vogue in recent years and they certainly are beautiful animals to keep but successful breeding requires a large enclosure with

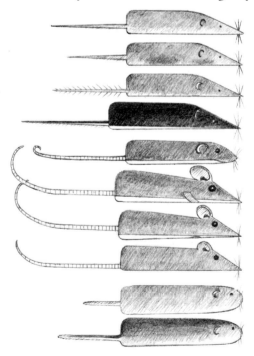

pygmy shrew
  tail length equals distance
  of ear to end of body
immature common shrew
  tail length equals distance
  of shoulder to end of body
white-toothed shrews
  no tooth pigment, long hairs
  on tail
water shrew
  large, very dark with stiff
  silver hairs on base of tail

harvest mouse
  diminutive, prehensile tail,
  ears small

yellow-necked mouse
  large ears and eyes, throat
  colour extensive, lively

wood mouse
  very common, small throat
  patch only

house mouse
  even, drab colour, smaller
  ears and eyes

field vole
  blunt nose, small ears,
  short tail, even colour

bank vole
  often red brown on back,
  tail dark above

Figure 21 Points of identification for commonly confused small mammals in simple exaggerated diagram form. See field guides for detail and tooth patterns.

Figure 23 Pygmy shrews have the long, highly sensitive nose typical of insectivores.

very dense cover left undisturbed. Much is made of the prehensile tail of the harvest mouse; however, if you catch house mice in your kitchen and put them in a vertical tank with branches and deep cover, you will find they are also very able at climbing along even narrow twigs and use their tails to steady themselves and grip with a similar dexterity. Do not feel you have to keep the more unusual small mammals to see interesting behaviour. House mice are more, shall we say, scented than harvest mice, but if well cared for all this is tolerable.

My mice usually come from our loft, caught in Longworth live traps. Three species come in from the adjoining barn: the house mouse, wood mouse and yellow-necked mouse. As an experiment I have kept all three of the smaller species found in the roof in one enclosure and they all lived well together until released. There was a particular sympathy between the dominant yellow-necked mouse and the house mice pair, but the wood mice kept to themselves more. You are more likely to get conflict between individuals of the same species and sex.

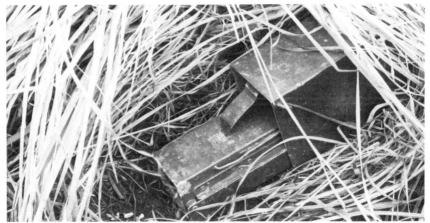

Figure 22 A Longworth small mammal trap painted dull green and set with bait on a vole run. The grass has been pushed aside to show the location.

The Longworth live traps are remarkable. You can tell how veteran a mammalogist is by his 'shock horror' inflation story about the price of these traps. When I first ordered mine they were 12/6, but on arrival they had gone up to 15/–. I still have my original five in regular use and the price at the time of writing of over £6–00 is still good value. You must always approach the capture of wild animals with the greatest care for their welfare: so much distress can be caused. Read up the subject, see others use the traps first and attend field courses if you can.

Half the skill of trapping lies in selecting the small mammal runs with

Figure 24 A hedgehog forages on a lawn at dusk.

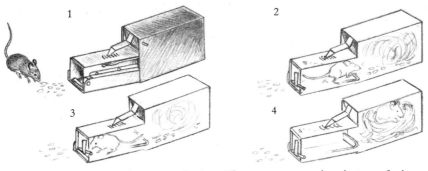

Figure 26 The Longworth trap mechanism. The mouse approaches the trap, feeds on some of the bait at the entrance and enters the tunnel activating the trigger. It approaches the bedding and food. The door now closed, the mouse finds its escape blocked. It feeds, sleeps and attempts to open the door until it is released.

care, so make sure that the particular run you select is being used. The set of the door is also vital: I have known traps put down without thought of whether small mammals use a run and with doors set open on such an insensitive trip that the mice or voles would have had to do press-ups on the bar to capture themselves. Place some cover over the trap and leave a small heap of food outside the tunnel entrance. After eating a few seeds the small mammals usually hop straight inside the newly arrived tunnel. Insulation is one of the most important considerations when the animal has gone into the nest-box section. Dense grass bedding is essential for this together with a surplus of food. In hot weather add a slice of apple to give moisture and a small bottle cap of fresh soft dog or cat food meat to prevent shrews from starving to death. My own traps have survived nearly twenty years of use because I painted the aluminium a dark green to reduce the chance of them being stolen.

There are other types of home-made box traps you can try with varying degrees of success. I have made several different types, but it is the Longworths which I rely on. Some establishments may allow you to borrow sets of traps and the Mammal Society has a trap loan scheme (see Appendix III). You must book well ahead and pay the price of carriage, but it can be most useful for a concerted week or fortnight's trapping session. I like to check the traps every few hours, although morning and evening is safe as long as all the captured animal's needs have been provided for.

When a more scientific approach is required the traps are set on specific grid lines and in this way clear divisions of species related to habitat can be shown. It is, incidentally, unforgivable to leave a trap set and lost by forgetting its location. Certain techniques enable the watcher to estimate population density, the movement of small mammals and behavioural changes throughout the year. This goes beyond our scope of general watching techniques, but in the case of small mammals it is

Figure 25 Juvenile greater horseshoe bats remain in the summer roost while most adults (one only is left in the apex of the roof) are away feeding.

relatively easy to handle, measure and familiarise ourselves with the different species by safe capture methods. Each trap represents a 'trap night', so although my five traps will take ten days to produce fifty trap nights, the trouble of obtaining and setting fifty traps in one night may only be worthwhile for special study reasons. Do remember that the time spent on the hands and knees setting the traps and the way you have set the door trip will make all the difference in your success rate.

# Mole

It is odd that the mammal species most easily recorded in distribution surveys is one of the most difficult to observe. Encounters with moles are usually confined to brief glimpses of individuals crossing roads or paths at high speed. The anatomy, which is so suited to digging and moving along tunnels makes it a clumsy running mammal and it seems to swim across the ground in a frenzy of wiggles; the live specimens I have handled are powerful wrigglers to say the least. If you move very quietly around woodland however you can come across surface tunnels being dug and patience can be rewarded with scenes of tunnelling. I watched one this spring as it worked away with characteristic abrupt heaves at the leaf litter; in half an hour it had extended its run by two metres.

Discussing such an elusive yet common subject, I tend to remember these occasional episodes when I have actually watched moles at work.

Figure 27 This shows clearly the contrast between ordinary molehills and the large breeding fortress in well wooded pasture.

Once when I had stopped to photograph deer tracks on a woodland path, I was joined by a mole which appeared at the legs of my tripod digging across the same path. The soil fell away and a pink nose appeared. Very mobile, twitching to and fro, the head looked out as the mole continued to push up the roof of its surface tunnel and extend its run across the path.

You may come across the actual mounds being excavated and it is worth waiting patiently next to an area of pasture which has recently been colonised. The most favoured habitat is damp woodland where the tunnels become established earthworm traps around which the mole tours for regular meals. When the surplus population is forced out into garden and grassland habitats the formation of the tunnels can be seen more easily. The enormous breeding hills or fortresses are impressive structures and Peter Stafford has taken photographs of the nest and young inside. I once found two freshly dug breeding hills on the same April day, 24 kilometres apart, which suggests that the timing of their breeding is very closely linked across their range. I have never dug into one myself, but if you know of a fortress hill which a farmer or gardener is about to destroy it would be well worth carefully opening the soil up first.

Moles are still subject to control (with poison and steel traps these days) because when they are numerous on farmland their hills may damage mower blades during haymaking, the runs can disrupt seedlings on the drill lines and extra harrowing may be required because of their workings. Mole catchers (still employed in places) have various ways of jumping placing their feet on either side of the surface-working mole and then digging rapidly to throw it out onto the grass. The mole catchers' thin willow rods which were used to hold the snares in their runs and were bent over to spring out the captured mole, were partly responsible for the willow-lined rivers and streams of East Anglia. The rods took root after the mole catcher moved on and if left by the field border, stood a chance of survival to grow into mature trees in the damp marginal land, which the moles themselves favoured for tunnelling.

## Shrews

Shrews are abundant everywhere and are particularly noticeable on summer walks along overgrown hedgerows and ditches. Their high-frequency squeaks can be heard at all times of day and their activity periods often involve disputes or group reaction. The squeaks come over very clearly on a bat detector (see Chapter 4) and the use of one may help locate shrews when one's ability to hear the high-frequency sounds has diminished.

When looking for shrews there are a few basic points to remember. Croin Michielson (see Further reading) has shown with Longworth trapping that common shrews are generally active underground in winter whereas the less abundant pygmy shrews remain on the surface at this time of year. This helps the two insect-eating species avoid direct competition when food is in short supply. Both types of shrew can be found under sheets of corrugated iron or under old water tanks left out in the countryside. Many people have difficulty in differentiating between juvenile common shrews and pygmy shrews and I have therefore included a simple set of diagrams (figure 21) to give a quick guide to the different features. In pygmy shrews the tail length must be the same as the length of the body from the base of the tail to the top of the head. In common shrews the tail is that much shorter in proportion to the body, only measuring up to the neck. In dead specimens it is easy to check the teeth and the recent field guides show the differences clearly.

Water shrews are very different animals. You may be lucky enough to get them living round your garden pond, but I have also caught them in Longworth traps well away from ponds and streams. Apart from their large size and sooty black colour, the distinct demarcation of the tail into black on top and white below is very obvious. This colouring is typical of an aquatic animal. We have two races of shrew in the Channel Islands both of which lack the red pigment in the teeth so obvious in our previously described types. The greater and lesser white-toothed shrews are distinguished by the tooth pattern as well as the tooth colour, the proportionately larger ears and distinct, long hairs which stand out from the otherwise typically hairy shrew tail. See the *Handbook* for the detailed differences of dentition.

I have kept common shrews for short periods of time. My first was found by a neighbour in a packing case and it revived on dog meat just in time. I enjoyed watching it establish the runs round its soil-based enclosure. The runs become so familiar to shrews that they do not stop to study the route and there is a favourite trick performed on captive shrews where a matchbox is introduced to the path. When the shrew bumps into this it inspects the new object with its complex of whiskers on its highly sensitive, long nose and jumps over. The new routine is then established and the ruthless observer then removes the matchbox to see the shrew still jumping over an imaginary obstacle. The tiny eyes clearly have limited use in the search for food whereas the whiskers are essential.

One memorable scene I came across when mammal watching occurred next to an old bridleway where traveller's joy merged with brambles and blackthorns. The ground flora under the thorns was fairly open but low branches, including many dead ones, lay about the leaf litter. I was attracted by the noisy squeaking and rustle of leaves and found myself watching an amazing scene of shrews in full flight, racing around a regular path in the lower parts of the thorn thicket. It seemed to be a family party but it was impossible to tell who was chasing who because the eight or ten shrews were fairly evenly spaced out. They were on the leaf litter part of the time, but then ran up branches to join with other parts of the lower tree stems. It seemed to go on for more than a minute but I am not sure. Whether it was a celebration of puberty or something similar I cannot say. I have never seen the classic tail grip where a mother leads her family, each shrew following, holding in its mouth the tail of the one in front, but having seen our polecat kittens follow their mother and each other closely in line across our lawn in this way (although not actually holding tails), I can quite believe the scene occurs frequently (see figure 100).

For a guide to shrew study you cannot do better than read Konrad

Lorenz's chapter on keeping water shrews in an aquarium in *King Solomon's Ring* (see Further reading). In my opinion this is one of the best books ever written on the relationship between Man and animals.

# Voles

I have never found the bank or field voles I have kept in captivity as absorbing or entertaining to watch as the wood mice described earlier. Field voles in particular, however, do make nests readily under sheets of

Figure 28 A small piece of corrugated iron in long grass is lifted to reveal this layout of field vole runs with the latrine on the left and two nests, one with young inside.

metal or wood left out on rough grass and you can see latrines, runs to and from nests and the nests themselves all mapped out in front of you when the once secure 'roof' has been lifted.

I tried to get better pictures of field voles for this book by lifting sheets of corrugated iron left on rough grass in a corner of the garden. I had

Figure 29 Bank voles climb freely through thickets in daylight and may nest high up in suitable cover.

camera and flashgun ready but despite discovering two nests the escape route was too effective – only a glimpse of a vole. The very same day, without my camera, I went to one of our beehives to adjust the large board we keep in front of the entrance and, on lifting it up, there sat a fine, fat field vole, staring up at me next to its nest. As usual I said 'Oh bother' and left it at that. The frustrations of mammal photography.

Bank voles are active in woodland during the day and if you watch at a hedgerow or wood regularly, you will be familiar with them. Unlike the field voles which are lost amongst the long grass in their hidden runs for much of the year, bank voles follow surface routes and will nest above ground, quite high up in foliage. Both species can turn up in each other's more typical habitat during trapping surveys. In my outdoor, free-range small mammal enclosure I found that bank voles were the most tame and easily watched visitors to the feeding site. Field voles tended to keep to the grass cover and retrieve food nervously. The larger island race of vole, the Orkney or Guernsey vole is only found on these islands in Britain. They favour depressions in the Caluna heath and make long established pathways out from main central runs in the bog and mosses. S. Wallis has worked on this species and reports some concern for the Orkney voles due to the growing development on hitherto neglected corners of rough heathland.

Figure 30 Observation of water voles on streams, rivers and canals is simplified by the use of a screen amongst reeds, sedges or trees on an opposite bank.

Our widespread large vole is the aquatic water vole and if you watch quietly along secluded river banks, they are active in daytime and particularly so in early evening. The familiar 'plop' of a diving water vole is often the first indication of the mammal as you walk by a river or stream. The latrines and feeding sites are very obvious, but tunnel entrances can be subterranean as well as at water level on the banks. When I have watched both brown rats and water voles, the rats seemed to use the more exposed sections of bank whereas only an occasional water vole would swim past. The voles favoured the more overgrown entrances in cuttings and the more dense the marginal flora, the more they seemed to prefer this type of habitat. The effect of mink predation on water voles is discussed in Chapter 7. If it is difficult to get to secluded water vole sites, the field vole is probably the best vole to watch because of its abundance in all types of environment.

## Mice and rats

Mice are generally more strictly nocturnal than voles or shrews, although I have watched wood mice in daytime in woodland. One once moved through ground flora past me looking very relaxed and healthy although it was midday. There was no sign of a ground predator having disturbed it from cover. The tail is held straight out when running and also when climbing and is clearly an important balance to the rapidly moving animal. Baited sites in woodland quickly attract wood mice and limited watching with torchlight is possible, as I found indoors with my captive colony. I have already devoted a great deal of space to this species, which is our most common mammal.

Yellow-necked mice often seem to turn up near buildings and at one farm in north Hertfordshire, a colony showed a preference for chutney in the farm kitchen. The first one I discovered as a boy was at the base of an old oak tree and I disturbed it from a hole in daylight. It was much larger and more vigorous than a wood mouse although externally, apart from the yellow throat band, it looked very similar. I caught it in a jam-jar and was most impressed at the yellow chest showing through the glass. I found that an individual from our loft opened up hazelnuts with a similar pattern to that of the wood mouse, but the nuts had much more indented, uneven sides. However, more experiments with different individuals should be made before this can be considered as a means of identification. Colonies occur locally and I have had as many as six individuals in our loft at one time. Greenhouses, sheds and dining rooms have all yielded records of yellow-necked mice in our area of Hertfordshire.

The attractive little harvest mouse and its famous round nest constructed amongst grasses above ground has by tradition been labelled 'rare' or 'declining due to modern farming techniques'. However in lowland Britain you will usually find the nests in wetland habitats. To watch at them, read up the books on the mouse, (two by Dr Stephen Harris have appeared recently, *The Secret Life of the Harvest Mouse* and *The Harvest Mouse* in the Mammal Society series, see Further reading), then explore the wetland sedges and high grasses very carefully. The mice particularly like to nest where high, long-leafed plants clump together and if you spot a female rushing away or dropping from a nest, it is most likely that

Figure 31 Reed warbler nests (left) may be found in similar habitats to those of harvest mice and are about the same size but woven around stems and open at the top. The harvest mouse weaves a nest of the actual living plants and grasses, completely enclosed (middle). Dormouse nests (right) are approximately twice the volume and pieces of available vegetation are woven in to give a soft inside, often of rose bay willow herb and bark strips.

you have found an occupied breeding nest site. My best views have been on the Essex Marshes where dense weed growth on the edge of wheat has concentrated the population. At one of our Hertfordshire sites, the numbers built-up to such an extent that John Tomkins, who discovered the site, was able to see many mice running away through the thin winter ground cover as he walked through. These population explosions are followed, as with voles in grassland, by 'crashes' and low numbers for some years until they build up again.

House mice are not very popular as subjects for watching mammals go. I have, as already mentioned, found them absorbing captive subjects, but the traditional reaction is to leap onto a stool, shriek and throw saucepans at these interesting mammals. I must admit to having been surprised by one myself which woke me up at 2.30 a.m. one morning in our bedroom. I put the light on and with blurred vision attempted to pick it up. It leapt clean over my arm and I was really startled. So I do have sympathy with the housewife shocked at such a lively small mammal in her own habitat. In Hertfordshire a survey of house mouse and brown rat control visits by East Herts District Council showed how these species come into human habitation especially in autumn as the colder weather commences, (Clark and Summers, 1980).

The black or ship rat occurs in a few local sites where port or dock warehouses provide a safe retreat. An inland locality was reported in the 1950s at Ware in mid-Hertfordshire although the canalside warehouses may no longer have populations. If you can find a site and can gain permission to watch at night in the warehouse or food store, the rats may be tolerant of torchlight.

All these mammals which associate closely with Man and cause much damage to food stores are subject to control and much as I enjoy watching

Figure 32 A black or ship rat showing the hairless ears which, with the eyes, are relatively larger than those of brown rats. The longer, spiky guard hairs also show up well here.

our resident brown rat population, there is a great risk of disease transmitted from the rats to humans or domestic animals. We live next to an orchard, outbuildings and a barn and have food out for deer and chickens so brown rats are always in evidence. They have done an amazing amount of damage from chewing the handles of a lawn-mower and making a series of holes in a coiled hose pipe so that it was unusable to attacking chickens from underneath as they roosted. They are easy to watch at dusk in early summer when their activity is at its height. If a feed hopper and water are present, different colonies from all around will visit regularly. Distinct paths are made and large or small rats come running up from different directions to retrieve food or eat on the spot.

One group of rat holes which I discovered under a shed had been excavated like a miniature badger set with large spoil heaps outside the entrances. I have seen rats getting water from a half-full bucket by hopping onto the edge, pausing, and then leaning down inside so that just their hind legs and tails were showing, still gripping the edge. When they are nervous, rats seem to scamper in quick bursts and old, confident ones appear to move along keeping their bodies very low to the ground. Refuse tips and the edges of waterways, particularly those near agricultural food dumps, are good places to watch rats and I have observed them at length on the tidelines in sea marshes where food remains could regularly be found.

Fat or edible dormice were introduced to Britain in 1902 at Tring Park in Hertfordshire and it is in this general area without great extension of their range where you are most likely to encounter them in the wild.

Figure 33 Edible dormice are often noisily active in woodland where they occur.

They can be heard in the trees at dusk when badger watching in Ashridge, for example, and resort to old hollow trees and house roofs. Although they hibernate, the ones I kept were active into late November and broke hibernation in a hard frost during January. They can breed late and we had young born on 9th October.

The indigenous common dormouse also seems often to breed late and young on a local nature reserve were born towards the end of September. The breeding nests are larger than those of the harvest mouse, but can be found at similar heights above the ground of up to a metre or more. If the harvest mouse breeding nest is like a cricket ball, the dormouse breeding nest can be up to the size of a small football.

Elaine Hurrell's recent book *The Common Dormouse* in the Mammal Society series describes the skill with which these mice can run through the branches and canopy of trees such as hazel in coppice. They jump from branch to branch in places they are familiar with and this is probably typical of most mammals which climb. They also freeze in the way so common with mice when they fear detection, and if you find the old oak, hornbeam, hazel and bramble type of habitats where these beautiful mice survive, watching at twilight can give results. Honeysuckle is often associated with these areas and a group of dormice has been seen at dusk climbing over a large honeysuckle in a garden in south Hertfordshire. My colleague Clive Banks came across a group in an area of typical mixed hedgerow vegetation, largely of brambles. It was one of those rare sightings when a whole family is dispersing from a nesting site. He said that for a few minutes the mice seemed to be everywhere he looked. John Tomkins (mentioned earlier in connection with harvest mice) found a young dormouse in a refurbished wren nest (12th October) about 1.8 metres above ground level. The nest was in a small elder with wild rose in deciduous woodland and the dormouse emerged when the

Figure 34 Above: Harvest mice are completely at home in stems and grasses above ground. The prehensile tail is constantly in use. Below: Dormice have a flat-footed look but are also very agile along branches and twigs in cover.

nest was touched gently. Even though the mouse was viewed from only one metre away, it climbed round the bush and returned to the nest. This behaviour was repeated on successive visits on 18th and 25th October. By 6th December the nest had been enlarged and the mouse was hibernating. The scrub habitat was fifteen to twenty years old and the dominant trees were birch and hornbeam. This type of secondary growth following clearing or coppice in old woodland is the ideal sort of site to look for dormice.

# Hedgehog

It is difficult to fit hedgehogs into any particular category of mammals. They are not 'small mammals' in the usual sense of the title, but like their fellow insectivores, the shrews and moles, hedgehogs are fierce consumers of various invertebrates. Their teeth are sharp and break up the shells of small snails as well as the less strong exoskeletons of ground beetles, millipedes and woodlice. Earthworms and slugs are consumed in quantities in suitably damp conditions so as to make these fascinating mammals popular with gardeners.

Hedgehogs are most easily encountered and watched in the suburban garden. I first saw the noisy and protracted courtship of two hedgehogs outside our back windows at home and followed a family of juveniles trailing behind their mother as a boy. They were walking under dense blackthorn thicket in an adjoining farm orchard. Our present garden is fenced in beyond the considerable climbing powers of hedgehogs and I miss not seeing them around at dusk. However, in the orchard outside the garden we can find them in the grass and the last one I saw this year allowed me to turn her over and find she was lactating. She seemed too preoccupied with motherhood to allow my brief interference to make her curl up. Normally hedgehogs freeze and contract for as long as they sense danger.

The spines and ability to curl up in a strong defensive ball are the

Figure 35 On disturbance, spines erect on the hedgehog which will tense and roll up until it becomes a complete and protected ball of spines.

features we most associate with hedgehogs. These mobile spines are an extraordinary adaptation of the mammalian hair and the powerful muscle which covers the back is made up of thin strands of fibre which contract rapidly on disturbance. The size of the muscle presents problems during dissection, as I have found, but when I have left road casualty hedgehogs at our badger set for them to eat, the badgers clean the skins beautifully to a neat, inside-out flat skin with just the spines left, face down.

On one occasion we were given a hedgehog which had been reared

Figure 36 Hedgehogs swim well, but garden swimming pools can be deadly traps unless an escape route is provided.

from the day it was found as an abandoned juvenile. Before we let it free-range, we learnt much of the variety of sounds hedgehogs can make. The courting couple I had observed snuffled and screamed, which is how I had noticed them initially. The tame hedgehog, 'Chog', was very amorous when introduced to a mate in our deer pen. He growled and churred a great deal and at other times when threatened by dogs or irritated, did mock jerking movements as he snorted. He swam well and even took a dip in a sea pool when on holiday with us.

The ectoparasites are a nuisance when we come into close contact with hedgehogs, but insect repellent powders are effective and with practice ticks can be quickly pulled off. I prefer this method to using matches, lighter fuel and similar 'infallible' methods which can be very difficult to apply. A quick nip with the fingers will catch the tick by surprise and remove its head. A dab of witch hazel will help heal the wound.

I do not recommend captivity for hedgehogs, even in large gardens, because they always want to escape and will pace round the perimeter. It is better to watch the free-range animals coming to feed on the lawn. Their well-documented habit of doing strange circles in open areas is not unusual, although difficult to explain. I have always thought this was associated with courtship, but listeners have written to the *Living World* radio programme describing hedgehogs doing this on their own night after night. Clockwise and anti-clockwise directions are used without particular bias.

Hedgehogs certainly like to keep to well used routes and road casualties occur repeatedly at certain sites. As soon as you note road deaths over the years, you will see generation after generation falling victim to vehicles at the same crossing points.

Dusk is certainly the prime watching time and in woodland I have turned my bat detector onto a pair snuffling through grass on a path. The detector picks up the sounds of the wandering hedgehog most effectively and makes following very easy with the amplified sound. Public parks and open spaces such as golf courses are ideal hedgehog viewing sites. Quiet walks with the binoculars (and bat detector if you have one) will eventually locate individual or sometimes groups of hedgehogs in favoured places. Gardens do seem to produce greater populations than farmland because of the abundance of lawns and retreats such as hedges and compost heaps. Tony Soper illustrates a hedgehog nest-box in his *The Bird Table Book* (see Further reading) and it is easy to encourage existing visitors with a bowl of milk at dusk and a suitable retreat such as this.

Having lived with a hedgehog indoors and out, I can confess to a deep prejudice in their favour. With grey squirrels, for most people they are our most easily watched mammal in towns and gardens away from open countryside and you can make observations virtually from your back windows.

# 4 Bats

It is sad that bat watching and bat study in general should be such a neglected area of wildlife observation. Stephen's excellent book *Watching Wildlife* which includes much on mammals, neglects the subject altogether. Warner's delightful book *Mammal Photography and Observation* only gives brief information on bats over two pages. There are references to bat photography in various books (mostly on studio work) and a certain amount of professional research work is also in progress. The amateur is however easily put off by the books which say that bats are difficult to identify, even in the hand, and impossible to distinguish on the wing. Apart from the odd specimen which turns up in any naturalist's activities, these fascinating mammals usually remain an enigma.

You have to go back to J. G. Millais and his *The Mammals of Great Britain and Ireland* (1904) to find real enthusiasm for bat watching so obviously enjoyed by his correspondents as well as by himself. The naturalists of the day confirmed their observations with cartridges loaded with dust shot, fired from shotguns. This often damaged the specimen and must have left many bats to fly away injured. Many more must have been lost because a bat falling to the ground in the dark and amongst dense summer flora is easily lost. I have a letter from Miller Cristy dated 1909 to Charles Oldham describing an old method of taking bats using the heads of burdock, hung in groups made white with meal on a pole: 'At this, they fly and are held by the hooked scales of the calices'. My colleague Ralph Newton once found a dead pipistrelle with its wing membrane caught up on a burdock, but I cannot otherwise vouch for this old capture technique. I certainly would not want anyone to try it out. Thankfully we have modern alternatives, although the shotgun is still used, sometimes with devastating results in bat roosts in the tropics.

Millais obviously determined to make up the gaps in his knowledge of bats and strengthen the content of his monumental three volume work in this area. The result, combined with the magnificent illustrations by George Lodge (1860–1953), provides us with an invaluable record of bat behaviour, well worthy of reference for the modern mammal watcher. Millais' original 'duty' to fill a gap of study for his book clearly became a consuming enthusiasm. (Main libraries should be able to make a copy of these large volumes available for reference.)

In our survey of mammals in Hertfordshire a similar sense of failure

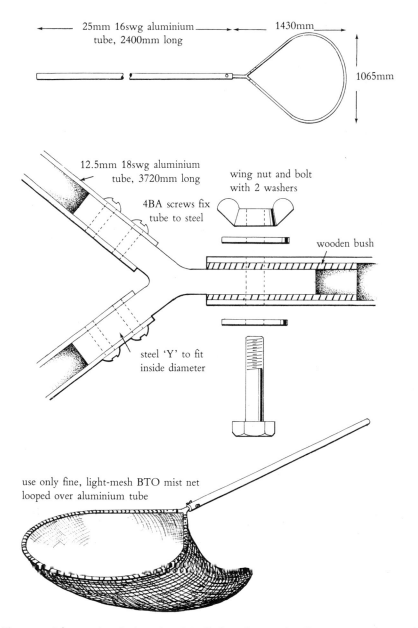

25mm 16swg aluminium tube, 2400mm long

1430mm

1065mm

12.5mm 18swg aluminium tube, 3720mm long

wing nut and bolt with 2 washers

4BA screws fix tube to steel

wooden bush

steel 'Y' to fit inside diameter

use only fine, light-mesh BTO mist net looped over aluminium tube

Figure 37 A bat net (mark 4) made originally by Clive Banks, illustrated here by Nigel Price.

over this branch of mammals (very evident in blank distribution maps published) encouraged the development of capture techniques. Pebbles can lure bats. I have flicked a small pebble 10 metres up to one bat flying over a wide lawn and brought it swooping down after the stone to flutter almost on the grass. Success at luring bats depends a great deal on the size of the pebble, possibly its colour, the degree of light and probably other individual factors such as food preference and hunger. It is difficult to send a small, beetle-sized pebble up to a high-flying bat and even if the object appears to be placed just right, well in the field of sonar location, many bats seem to sense that it is artificial. We probably underestimate how much bats use their eyes and 'blind as a bat' is one of the most inaccurate similes ever.

There is an excellent description of echolocation by bats in Yalden and Morris', *The Lives of Bats* (1975). It is a highly complex subject in itself and involves the frequency, wavelength harmonics and amplitude of sound. The hunting sounds made by bats are above the range of human hearing although they squeak during flight and to each other within our range. All the European bats make pulses of sound at frequencies of up to 100,000 hertz or cycles per second (Hz). Our limit of hearing is about 20,000 Hz and this level tends to decrease with our advancing age. An insect is located when the sounds sent out by the bat are reflected back in the form of an echo. About ten pulsed sounds are made each second and bats 'read' the echoes in great detail. Some moths have developed sounds which effectively 'scramble' the bat's echolocation and dive out of the way to evade the approaching night predator.

Handkerchieves knotted at the corners have been known to divert low-flying bats and may even engulf the attracted animal. Fly-fishing at dusk often lures bats feeding over water, although the swish of the line as much as the artificial fly tied to the end may be the cause of the deception. The hand net uses a method of rapid confusion to capture a flying bat. Bats are so efficient at avoiding nets or sticks (Millais wrote of his frustration at using a fly-fishing rod and a butterfly net), that only a skilful flick of the light mesh mist net in following the flight of the bat entangles the mammal. It must not be used tennis-racket style, but carefully, with a rapid wrist action. Once the flight is interrupted by the swish of the net, the hoop stands a chance of enclosing the bat. I find that the air disturbance caused by the action of the net to and fro emulates the movement of insects, and draws bats within reach for attempts at capture.

With colleagues I have caught and handled over 800 bats in the past

Figure 39 A portrait of another *Myotis* bat, the natterer's. Note the adaptation of forearm, thumb and fingers to the wing structure, the sharp teeth and the ears with the long tragus.

Figure 40 Leisler's bats have the same type of ear structure as noctules and strong shoulders, but they are smaller and lack the copper-brown hue to the hairs.

five years and the net is useful when held under roosts (see figures 37 and 42). Capture by hand net must only be contemplated after consultation with the Nature Conservancy, (see Appendix III). Permission for mist netting is also needed and any projects involving tagging bats needs a licence. Standing mist nets can be useful in some circumstances and are ideal in the tropics where there are far greater numbers of bats.

A bat in the hand can be examined, measured and identified in detail. Using the hand net, (first made by Clive Banks) we have been able to catch the second Nathusius' pipistrelle ever found in Britain. It was

Figure 42 Clive Banks using the mini bat detector at dusk and holding an aluminium bat net ready for use. A hand lamp is clipped to his chest which has two settings: 36 watt spot beam or 5 watt working lamp connected to a maintenance free lead acid rechargeable battery on a shoulder sling.

examined live at the British Museum (Natural History) with the use of a microscope at times, and released unharmed at the site of capture.

The battery powered bat detector, although more limited in use for identification than the hand net, is nonetheless a very useful modern aid to bat study. It works on the basis of tuning the frequency dial as the bat calls in flight. Bats hunt and navigate with their sound pulses which vary in intensity and harmonics, and bat detectors have been developed

Figure 41 A pipistrelle skilfully echolocates with its mouth open.

to tune to different frequencies and produce audible clicks and chirrups from the speaker. A microphone is directed at the flying bat and the operator adjusts the response dial, but as yet not all species can be distinguished from one another. You cannot, for example, split the noctule or Leisler's bats or the *Myotis* species. The long-eared and barbastelle species can only be heard within a metre or so, but in conjunction with the other methods of capture and handling I strongly recommend the use of a detector. It is now available in mini form, powerful, pocket-sized and much cheaper than the larger original types.

The following data is from J. H. D. Hooper's work (see Further reading) and is listed in the QMC mini detector handbook:

| Species | Sound heard from detector's loudspeakers | Tuning frequency for optimum response |
|---|---|---|
| Bechstein's Daubenton's Natterer's Whiskered | clicks | 45–50 kHz |
| Mouse-eared Barbastelle Long-eared Serotine | clicks | 40–45 kHz |
| Noctule Leisler's Serotine | chirrups | 20–25 kHz |
| Pipistrelle | chirrups | 45–50 kHz |
| Greater horseshoe | cheeps | 80–85 kHz |
| Lesser horseshoe | cheeps | 105–115 kHz |

(Long-eared and barbastelle bats may only be heard at close range.)

Used in conjunction with binoculars both hand nets and detectors are then two very important aids in identification. Bats are difficult to follow with field glasses although the light intensifier or infra-red types make it possible to see the rapid flights of moths and bats quite dramatically after dark. The cost of such equipment is however, prohibitive for the amateur at present.

As my theme is watching rather than identification, an answer to a complicated problem was to draw silhouettes of the different species for comparison, all in proportion to each other. It is no great help to repeat general data already available and accessible in other books but a brief summary of the British bat species seems worthwhile.

## Horseshoe bats family Rhinolophidae

Generally local with seven *Rhinolophus* species across the Palaearctic. Hang freely from walls and roofs when hibernating with wings surrounding body. Echolocate through nostrils with mouth closed. Hunt over regular areas, generally flying low (about six metres) and will alight to feed. Feed late with butterfly-like gliding flight. Can be active throughout night. Lesser horseshoe more rapid in flight than greater with erratic turns.

## Typical insect-eating bats family Vespertilionidae

The **mouse-eared bats** *Myotis* species are found throughout the world. Twenty-one species across the Palaearctic region. Echolocate with mouth open. Hibernate in crevices. Favour areas of water, as do most bats. All types of roosts.

### Whiskered bat *M. mystacinus* and Brandt's bat *M. brandti*
Very similar even when examined in the hand. Emerge with medium, often fast flight, broad wings, on regular routes at sunset. Daytime flights.

### Natterer's bat *M. nattereri*
Broad wings, steady flight round treetops particularly, repeated through night, over water, too; 'buzz' sound can sometimes be heard.

### Bechstein's bat *M. bechsteini*
Very rare, slow, late evening flight in woodland, usually low.

### Mouse-eared bat *M. myotis*
Very large, wide wings with slow, heavy flight over open country. Local on south coast of Britain, but widespread across Palaearctic.

### Daubenton's bat *M. daubentoni*
Broad wings, large feet, particularly favour ponds and old wooded areas. Circling, fluttering flight over water surface. Pipistrelles also numerous over water, but do not remain close to the surface in the same prolonged way.

### Serotine *Eptesicus serotinus*
Slow, steady flight with broad wings, usually solitary after dark. Regular routes, particularly on foliage edges. High flight initially, low later.

### Leisler's bat *Nyctaclus leisleri*
Drab brown and smaller when compared with noctule, similar fast flight with dives; early emergence. Daylight flights. (In the course of survey work these bats found at several sites in Hertfordshire so probably not as rare as often thought.)

### Noctule bat *N. noctula*
Usually the first bat to fly at sunset, often in parties; rapid flight, narrow wings, deep dives. Flies over rivers and lakes particularly. May travel long distances to feed. First flight about one hour in length.

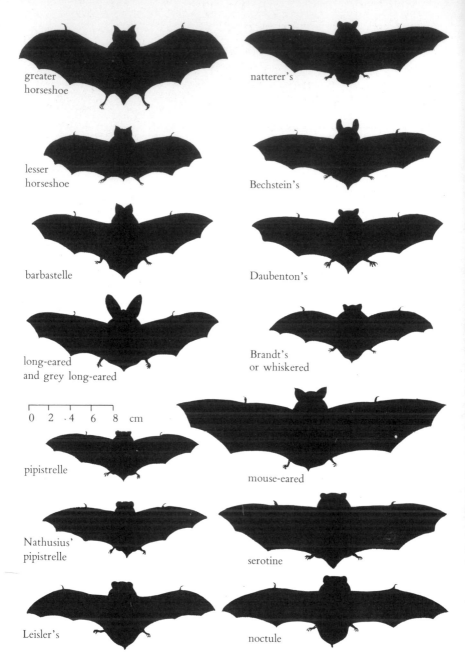

greater
horseshoe

natterer's

lesser
horseshoe

Bechstein's

barbastelle

Daubenton's

long-eared
and grey long-eared

Brandt's
or whiskered

0  2  ·4  6  8  cm

pipistrelle

mouse-eared

Nathusius'
pipistrelle

serotine

Leisler's

noctule

Figure 43 Bat silhouettes. Details of emergence and flight patterns which also help in indentification are given in the text.

**Pipistrelle** *Pipistrellus pipistrellus*
There are 10 to 12 *Pipistrellus* species across the Palaearctic. Small, difficult to distinguish from *Myotis* species; all types of flight, rapid, fluttering. Congregate over water particularly, feed throughout night with breaks. **Nathusius' pipistrelle** *P. nathusii* very rarely found in Britain. More aggressive, slightly larger than *P. pipistrellus*. Similar flight.

**Barbastelle** *Barbastella barbastellus*
Very local and elusive, solitary; frequents woodland and rivers. Very dark; ears meet on top of head. Variable emergence, active at different times throughout night. Low flight, heavy and fluttering, often over water.

**Long-eared bat** *Plecotus auritus*, **grey long-eared bat** *P. austriacus*
Both broad winged (latter local to southern Britain). Fairly late to emerge; frequent woods and gardens. Flights with breaks through night, first lasts about an hour. Worth getting up an hour before dawn to watch at large colonies.

Further information to help with identification can be found in field guides and the *Handbook*. These will give details of the tragus, or projection in front of the ear, which differs for each species. There is also a good section on the grey long-eared bat in *The Mammals of Pakistan* by Roberts (see Further reading).

As you get to know your bats, the enjoyment of watching develops. Bats are, indeed, remarkable in many ways. Few types of mammal watching can rival the pleasure of seeing a group of feeding noctules appearing at sunset as the swallows, martins and swifts begin to disperse. They are usually the first bats to appear and in high summer it is light enough to follow their rapid, powerful flight with binoculars. The thin, narrow wings are distinctive and all kinds of manoeuvres can be seen as the noctules pursue their insect prey.

Both noctules and serotines fly high initially but will come low as twilight turns into darkness. If you are standing still and quietly where a particular food item is prevalent, the bats will feed right round you. On one particular night on 23rd August I heard a clicking sound on the edge of a copse. (It is odd to hear bats before you see them.) I emerged from the trees to find five noctules feeding in the corners of two adjacent fields. My diary notes observe: 'They concentrated on the corner, about 10 metres up, swooping beautifully to pick off moths or dung beetles almost from the grass tops. The sound they made resembled that of rubbing your index and middle fingers together very rapidly to make the joints flick against each other.

'They would fly up with the prey and come past at head height, munching noisily. There were squeaks and some chasing suggesting courtships, but obviously the matter in hand was to eat the concentration of food rapidly. Perhaps a particular species of insect was hatching in large numbers there. It was a damp evening after heavy rain in the morning and afternoon.

'The cattle saw me and came charging over to stand wheezing, snorting and jumping, but the bats took no notice and a noctule flew just over the back of one. It was such a rushed, busy feeding scene with swoops, dives and direct rapid flights, so unlike the behaviour of the more sedate serotines. Serotines generally feed alone, but even when I have seen and caught them in groups with noctules, they do not seem to have the same sense of urgency. I checked the time and it was 8.45 pm.'

The following night I returned to see if the groups would turn up again at the same time. My diary records: 'It was warm, dry and still. No noctules appeared, only my lone serotine on its usual beat over the orchard hedge, along the edge of the copse and back. The high-frequency calls it made beyond the range of the human ear, came over beautifully on the bat detector, up to 30 metres distant and very loud when circling me. I wonder why the noctules are not interested tonight? It suggests that they know the suitable feeding conditions for a particular part of their home range in certain weather conditions. It may be that they do not even explore some areas. On emergence, the older bats could from experience go to a part of their territory where food is most likely to be found. The younger bats would learn by the experience of the older ones.'

On 22nd July 1978 I watched a group of four noctules flying for about ten minutes feeding over a wheat field as if inside a gigantic enclosure. They all flew back and forth within the exact limits of the five hectare field, never crossing the road boundary on the south side, or entering woodland or orchard on the other sides. I was not able to discover what insect food was hatching from or flying above the wheat.

At a site in the Lea Valley together with two colleagues I have caught a number of flying serotines and noctules, finding that serotines will feed

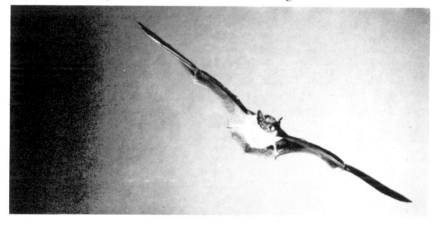

Figure 44 After initial high flights at dusk, serotines settle to hunt on steady, direct flight paths with intermittent soaring.

out quite soon after the appearance of the noctules. They feed together and as darkness increases are difficult to distinguish, even with binoculars. The flight pattern of the serotines then settles to a steady, regular beat up and down woodland or hedgerow edges, particularly over pasture. At first they will be just as acrobatic in pursuit of prey in the air as the noctules, but normally break away from the group and become solitary after dark. Even then, a clear view against a light night sky will show the distinctive broad-winged silhouette. The flight is often low and as steady as a wide-winged model aeroplane being controlled in a straight flight path.

A study by Ralph Newton of a mixed roost of serotines and noctules over three seasons (1976–8) gave a clear picture of the relationship of these two species and their activities. He kept a careful watch, noting the numbers of bats emerging at dusk, the times of emergence and the weather conditions as well as taking details of all caught specimens. The noctules seemed to be an all-female pre-breeding roost which broke up at the end of May, but the female serotines were resident. The male serotines stayed there only in the spring and autumn. The noctules were noisy before and during emergence, especially so during the day in hot weather. In the summer, when the serotines were alone in the roost they were very quiet and departed to feed with little noise.

In temporary captivity the two species will also show their different personalities. Both are aggressive initially, but tame quickly. Serotines are beautiful bats to handle and watch, and noctules are handsome and boisterous. There seems to be little value in moving these large, strong flying bats from sites as they fly back huge distances when you release them. Both species are recorded to have flown in excess of a hundred miles and movements by noctules of over 1,000 miles have been recorded in Europe.

Figure 45 A serotine caught in a hand net just prior to release. Note the dark face with more delicate features than those of the noctule.

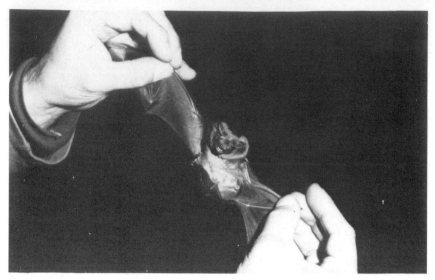

Figure 46 The noctule's powerful shoulders and long, narrow wings can be compared with the size of the hands. There is a gloss to the short, brightly coloured hair.

Confidence with the identification of bats on the wing comes with capture and handling as well as watching over a long period of time. For biological records, measured and examined bats are needed. With experience it is possible to identify noctules, serotines and Daubenton's bats on the wing. The smaller pipistrelles will dive down to the water's

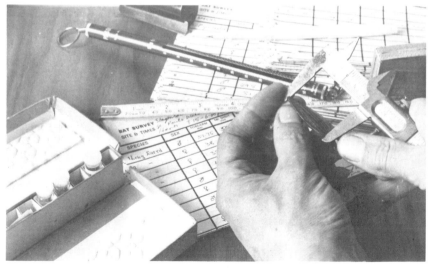

Figure 47 Standard measurements are taken of a bat: here the forearm length is noted. Ectoparasites may be collected in alcohol in small bottles.

surface and fly with the same hovering flight as the Daubenton's bats, but only for short periods. In work with colleagues, and by catching the bats to confirm our observations, we have found that in Britain only Daubenton's bats circle and hover right across a pond or lake as if tied to the water's surface by a thread. I have also watched them on saltings, hunting over the brackish water where a stream joined saltmarsh lagoons, and confirmed identification by capture. Some flights continued from lagoon to lagoon with swift detours over patches of dividing reeds. This behaviour is very like the surface feeding of swallows on a hot, still evening as the caddis fly larvae and mosquitos are hatching. It is as beautiful in a more delicate, precise way, as the dramatic, powerful flight of the noctules. If a slight movement by the watcher sends a ripple through the water, it seems to disturb the echolocation and the bats move off. Ralph Newton has observed that the Daubenton's bats can settle

Figure 48 The Daubenton's bat has large feet, a thick neck and short, dense hair when compared with similar sized *Myotis* bats. Tail membrane and tragus differences are the field signs to look for in the hand.

easily on water and take off. Pipistrelles will swim to the bank and climb out before taking flight. The large feet of Daubenton's bats appear to be ideal for catching the insect life at the water's surface and they probably 'pouch' or enclose prey in the wing membrane before bringing it up to the mouth to a lesser extent than similar species. The claws are like little fishing gaffs and it will be interesting to see what high speed flash photography can reveal of the bats' hunting techniques.

At the saltings site, as well as Daubenton's bats and pipistrelles, I have regularly watched noctules flying from a distant village across the marsh at a considerable height of about 40 metres. I could not distinguish any feature on the marsh but presume the attraction to the bats was to catch crickets and other large insects at a farm or town refuse tip in the distance. A flight of several miles to feed seems to be quite acceptable to noctules.

The Daubenton's bats were not observed over the sea, but left the saltmarsh waters to fly to a group of nearby wych elms. These appeared to be the summer roost in an otherwise very open area of flat farm fields with scattered single oaks. At a sewage farm site we failed to locate this species over the many lagoons despite hundreds of pipistrelles feeding each night and put this down to the lack of mature trees in the vicinity. Ponds and lakes in the same area, set in old parkland with wood and mature old trees, inevitably turned up this 'water bat'.

In towns or villages the small sparrow-sized bat you see flying about the houses and roosting in them is nearly always our common bat, the pipistrelle. They will fly low to good feeding sites and congregate at particularly good insect concentration as darkness increases. You can tell if a flight is a departure or return by the circling behaviour. They will fly and may circle once before departure, unless disturbed by the presence of hand nets but circle several times on return. One pipistrelle I watched outside a church tower flew in an L-shaped flight round two sides of the tower, apparently about to re-enter. However, it kept this flight pattern up for a quarter of an hour, just going back and forth alone. The only explanations I can think of are either courtship behaviour to a bat out of sight in the tower or a juvenile repeating newly learned flight manoeuvres. It is more usual to find bats in the body of a church rather than the draughty tower. They often fly above the pews, exit through remote hidden gaps and return to tuck away behind roof woodwork again.

Any areas of water are also likely places to watch pipistrelles, particularly if tree lined. The natterer's and whiskered bats fly higher as a rule and keep to the fringes of trees or bushes. With colleagues I have caught whiskered bats along with Daubenton's bats where both were coming through gaps in the foliage to feed at the water's edge. Daubenton's bats literally dive overhead out of woodland onto the surface of the water and then weave, often in groups of five or six, across the ponds. Ralph Newton has seen a group wheeling and chasing just like a screaming summer party of swifts, illuminated over the water by an angler's night light.

Fishermen will often cast and find a bat dips to the bait, sometimes even becoming caught up by the hook. Others have reported that the night alarm of the line is activated when a bat has alighted on the float or disturbed the line, probably picking it up in its claws for a short distance before discarding it.

Long-eared bats are fascinating to watch in their roosts. They favour the open, clean lofts of homes and it is well worth recording the movements of the clusters in relation to the time of day and temperature. They have very broad wings, enormous ears and are highly sensitive to nets. Feeding generally takes place in woodland where they can exploit dense foliage. Although the ears unfold and become very distinctive in flight, these bats are generally out too late for clear observation with binoculars. Even at close quarters they will avoid the hand net.

Oddly enough, it is the long-eared bat which most often seems to turn

Figure 49 Long-eared bats prefer to enter roof spaces and hang in clusters in the apex. Their ears fold back at rest but are fully extended in flight.

up in standing mist nets, set up at night by bird ringers. This is explained by their feeding behaviour. They alight on the ground as well as on foliage to catch prey and it seems certain that although well aware of the net, they are attracted to moths or other insects caught in the mesh. Having landed, they become entangled.

The horseshoe bats are intriguing whether in summer (the juveniles are remarkable) or during hibernation in winter. Concern for the greater horseshoe bat means that main hibernation caves are grilled to lock people out and the summer breeding sites are carefully protected. Disturbance at both times of year is critical and human presence has affected the populations in the past. Fluctuations in the numbers of mammals is most obvious on the outer limits of their distribution, but the greater horseshoe bat should be protected throughout its range. All kinds of reasons have been given for the decline and Dr R. E. Stebbings has reported their numbers as being only two per cent of the 1900 population in Britain. Human disturbance to caves and the loss of stable summer breeding sites has contributed to the fall in numbers, but modern research may identify precise reasons over the next few years. The conservation and management of all our bats is to be encouraged.

By special permission I have visited the hibernation caves in the Mendips and seen these bats with lesser horseshoes and smaller species. Whilst the horseshoe bats cluster or hang freely from the cave roof, the *Myotis* species tuck themselves into cavities and crevices. Exploring ice house hibernacula with colleagues I have found natterer's, whiskered and Daubenton's bats well hidden in cracks in the brickwork. Ice houses were built underground as cold storage areas for country houses and are usually domed and of brick cavity wall construction. (The *Myotis* species may prefer to live in tree roosts close to the food sources, and these bats are very elusive on the wing.) Disturbance at this time can mean that the bats use up too much energy and fail to survive the winter. Human body heat close to a hibernating bat can begin to rouse it. Should you see a bat you are watching move or sway slightly, step back and keep your distance. Cave and ice house access must always be obtained through the permission of the owners and you must kit yourself up

Figure 50 Greater horseshoe bats hang by their feet, their wings folded round the body throughout hibernation. These are in a winter cave but are still active and two have bands on their forearms.

properly. Lamps on helmets are essential as well as old clothes or a boiler suit. Enter such sites only with experienced guides, never under any circumstances go alone and as with watching in mountains and hill country, leave a route plan and time for return.

I have watched the horseshoes near a breeding roost in Avon and where these larger species can be confused, the bat detector is a very helpful piece of equipment. The ultrasonic frequency response for horseshoes is very distinct (see page 56) and their flight is more moth or butterfly-like than, say, that of the noctule or serotine.

All bats glide at some stage but it is a particular feature of horseshoe flight which is also surprisingly low. They favour *Gytropus* beetles and, like the long-eared bats, will freely land on the ground. Dr Stebbings describes the flight of the lesser horseshoe as having more rapid wing beats with erratic turns and glides, often very low to the ground.

Bats allowed to fly indoors demonstrate the superb powers of echolocation they possess and it is surprising how well they can alight on various surfaces. Long-eared bats with one or two trial approaches, can land upside down onto polystyrene ceiling tiles and cling, confidently surveying the strange environment. The general public, however, is very ignorant of bats and can get extremely upset by their presence indoors. One householder I came across pulled the end of the roof off his house extension in an effort to frighten off a colony of pipistrelles. Here, management rather than control is the answer and with the help of several colleagues I have made contact with the local Environmental Health departments and these divert complaints to us. We find this a

Figure 51 A lone natterer's bat hibernates in a limestone cave crevice.

good way of getting to know the behaviour of bats, their distribution, and of helping to conserve them.

If, when we have been called to a house by a distressed family, we cannot persuade the owner to keep the bats in his roof space, we retrieve and release them in alternative suitable sites. It is, however, very difficult to keep them in a particular place and after several days they move on. It is far better to leave bats where they are and if the owner wants to seal up the entrance and exit holes this can be done when the bats have changed roosts. They move about a great deal during the summer but are inactive from October to March apart from occasional flights.

Complaints most often occur at summer breeding roosts when as many as fifty to a hundred pipistrelles may breed as a separate female colony in a cavity wall. Modern houses are frequently badly finished and access to poorly capped walls or exterior wall tiles is relatively easy. The owner should be encouraged to leave the colony (it is only in the cavity wall as a rule, rarely in the loft space) and repair gaps in warped wood or masonry when the roost has changed. These are excellent sites for watching bats at dusk. All these activities familiarise the bat watcher

Figure 52 A popular temporary summer breeding roost of female pipistrelles is in south west facing cavity walls of modern houses as here.

with the different species and types of roost favoured.

Few of us are lucky enough to have bats in the roof but it may be possible to attract a colony to a box. A regular flight of bats to watch can give great interest in the summer and records of emergence, flight durations and changes in occupation can be kept. Boxes were first developed to give roosts in the extensive fir plantations established across so much of Britain in the last thirty years where old hollow trees had largely vanished and were also intended to provide roosts in urban areas when attached to the outside of houses. They give the bats a valuable,

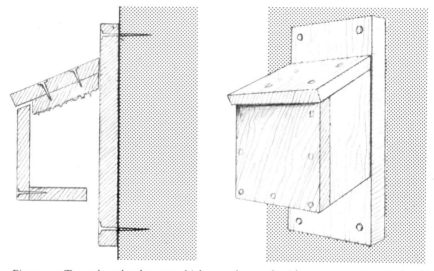

Figure 53 To make a bat box use thick, rough wood without preservative. It should be about 10 centimetres square inside. When the top section is pulled up the lid lifts off. Make sure you secure the box very firmly to a wall or tree and after three to four years the box may attract roosting bats.

dry retreat. Dr Stebbings has kindly forwarded the information on these boxes. He has found up to fifty bats in one ten centimetre cube box and it is best to offer several locations and aspects. We have found most bat roosts in houses are west and south facing. South facing boxes may suit summer breeding and north facing ones may be used for hibernation. Dr Stebbings has found that it may take three years before the bats accept the box. It is, therefore, important to weatherproof the timber as thoroughly as possible.

If local groups of mammal enthusiasts organised bat study with rescue schemes, an enormous amount of information would be added to our knowledge of the distribution of bats and much could be done to conserve the species present. The reward comes in the fun of visiting ponds, churches, ice houses, caves and even house roofs to see what species may be present.

# 5 Gnawers and nibblers

The larger mammals which gnaw and nibble at vegetation can be as damaging to Man's crops and food stores as the mice and rats. If you are a detached observer you can enjoy their behaviour without resentment, but the need for their management must be recognised. Being subjected to constant pressure from predators, camouflage and defensive strategies are highly developed in these mammals.

## Rabbit

I was once walking along a bank with an extensive rabbit warren dug into the side of it and had knelt down to crawl under a barbed wire fence, when I heard an eerie sound close by. It was as if a regular heartbeat was coming from the very earth. For a moment I was unable to trace the sound until I realised that the noise was coming from the nearest rabbit earth. A rabbit had detected me and was thumping out its back foot warning underground.

Rabbits tend to thump out warnings more readily at smaller predators than Man. The best display of fluffed up white tail bobbing and thumping I have witnessed was that of two rabbits next to a thicket when a black cat came stalking along towards me. They were unaware of me and kept their distance from the cat without actually running off. Many juvenile rabbits are taken by cats and predators of all kinds (see Chapter 7).

Although rabbits are now so widespread again after the initial

Figure 54 Rabbits around earth entrances.

devastating effects of myxomatosis it is surprising how few good photographs of wild rabbit colonies exist. The modern literature is quite extensive with Thompson and Wordon's *The Rabbit*, Lockley's *The Private Life of the Rabbit* and Cowan's *The Wild Rabbit*.

Rabbits principally feed out from their warrens and cover at dawn and dusk, but in quiet, undisturbed areas you can see them active throughout the day. Young rabbits often emerge in clusters, looking curious and uncertain at the warren entrances during warm afternoons. One certain time for watching them in the evening is after a heavy shower of rain. They always become active and feed after rain especially on a sunny evening. There is much to see in rabbit behaviour with the courtship chases, spray marking by males onto females with urine, (the highest compliment it seems to the chosen mate) and territorial disputes. Establishing social rank results in aggression and behaviour similar to that I describe in Chapter 6 with reference to muntjac deer. If you can examine a dead buck rabbit, look for the damp area of the gland under the chin which is used for scent marking. This becomes obvious when the animal leans forward, its throat flat to the ground, and it is used to reinforce social rank and territory on pasture. Such behaviour is easily spotted in grazing animals.

A two-year-old rabbit is an old rabbit and their reproductive fame is in response to heavy predation. I shall always remember Eric Ashby's superb film of a fox stalking through a rabbit warren and finishing the hunt with a final rush to capture its prey. Badgers tend to hunt by scent and just dig out the breeding stops (short, blind tunnels, resealed after the mother has fed her young), where the juvenile rabbits are born and where the does visit to feed them. You can sometimes find many dug out stops in large warren areas. If young rabbits are left strewn about uneaten, a cat is probably responsible rather than a fox or badger which will normally eat the whole litter.

The aggression of rabbits will be familiar to anyone who has kept them and we have a large wild one which dug into our Chinese water deer pen and made a burrow. On certain evenings it carefully approaches each deer in turn and reaches up until they are touching noses. Then it 'bounces' the deer and makes it run off with a sudden jump. After a short run round, it goes to another and repeats the performance. It appears, irrespective of the physical size of its substitute 'colony', to want to establish a group hierarchy.

Rabbits are large, easily available mammals to observe and watching around the warrens can show a complex life history. My best views have been from a high seat and when stalking quietly up to feeding areas at dawn. They seem to be at their most relaxed in the early hours of a midsummer's day, especially if the colony has fed safely and been undisturbed the previous evening.

Figure 56 A fine sika stag with the characteristic thick black mane is seen here in the autumn rut.

Confusion with hares is possible, but field marks on the ears and about the tail, the size of the animal and the relative length of the ears are all points of difference (see figure 58). Hares are mammals of the open fields and although you will often see them in woodland, the disturbed animal runs off with speed quite unlike the quick, tail up scuttle into cover or into an earth entrance of the rabbit.

Figure 58 Rabbits ears are shorter than the head length. Brown hare ears are equal to their head length with distinct black tips.

# Brown hare

The home of the hare is a very simple form of grass or stubble and Dr S. Tapper has shown in his research on the gradual decrease in the population that our hares have suffered (particularly since the 1960s), that numbers are at their greatest on arable land and that permanent grassland holds fewer. It is a great pity that these fine animals of the fields are becoming more and more local, although mild springs increase numbers. Night shooting, chemical poisoning especially by paraquat when used on stubble and the burning of stubble have all been put forward by Dr Tapper as contributing reasons for the decline. The highest population for this century was recorded in 1910 and the decline has been gradual to date. In Hertfordshire large numbers have been shot in single shoots, over the big open cereal farmland of the northern districts: as many as 200 in a day. In some areas they seem to be restricted to particular fields and to be absent from others.

Spring is the highlight of the year for hare watching when the 'mad March hares' court, box and chase in the open fields. The flat, crouched position in the form or when approached is characteristic and attractive. To examine their form it is possible to mark a disturbed hare as it runs

Figure 57 A menil coloured fallow buck with large, palmated antlers.

Figure 59 A hare form in stubble (left) and a hare lying out in long grass (right). Rabbits will also flatten in this way prior to escape from danger.

off. If, in stubble for example, you walk directly to the spot, keeping your eyes firmly fixed on the place where the animal ran off, you should locate the shallow structure (see figure 59). The young or leverets are not born naked in a stop like rabbits, but out in a form, too, with full body hair.

Our sheepdog once chased a half-grown hare and it showed the surprising speed and agility of the species as it avoided him. It got to a farm gate and raced underneath. This held the dog up somewhat (and me) and by the time I had reached the other side there was no sign of the hare, just a very confused dog. There was a low wooden bridge over the field drainage stream just the other side of the gate and I looked underneath. The young hare was crouched in the water, ears flattened back and eyes bright. It stared at me, more afraid of the dog above and I left it in peace. It had jumped from the bridge and the dog was still unable to locate the scent. As I walked on with the frustrated dog, I thought it odd that an animal of the open field should use such a tunnel-like retreat to hide in, but it had used water to lose its scent and the disappearing act had worked on the dog, so that knowingly or unknowingly it had very successfully used two excellent escape techniques.

Hares appear to keep very much within local areas without extensive

Figure 60 A spring congregation of hares with courtship stances and 'boxing' in progress.

movements or migrations. We caught one during an organised capture and release of wild deer for research near Hitchin and ear-tagged it with a request for return. The tag was given to the organiser, Dr Oliver Dansie, a year later having been taken from the hare after a shoot. The hare had been shot only a field away from where we had caught it and published accounts indicate that this is quite usual.

When you locate hares, a crawl can bring you up very close if hedge-row cover is available and watching from a vehicle can be very successful because hares tend to get used to tractors and land rovers in their habitats. In spring I have been so close in a vehicle that the hares must have been totally uninterested and preoccupied. The frolics and leaps make hares particularly impressive mammals to watch in the open fields. The behaviour of standing up on the back legs and boxing at each other is not unique to hares, but although I have seen foxes, rabbits, wood mice and red deer do this, it is a particular feature of courtship and rivalry between the hares. Their speed and leaping has made them a popular coursing animal from the earliest times with gazehounds, (lurchers, greyhounds and deerhounds), and beagles or bassets wear the hare down with prolonged pursuit: over a short distance there is no chance of capture, but as relentless tracking by scent continues, the hare gradually tires out.

## Mountain hare

I have watched the mountain hares in their white winter pelage in spring in Scotland, but the closest views of these 'blue' hares (blue in the mammal world is really a warm grey colour), I have enjoyed were on the golf links in Dublin when on a dawn foray to watch the hares amongst the sand dunes. When you are a lowland mammal yourself used to one type of hare only, you notice at once how much shorter the ears are when compared with those of the brown hare; the head seems blunter and the legs almost more gangling especially when compared with rabbits.

The Irish hare is a subspecies with slight variations on the Scottish type. The Scottish mountain hares have been introduced into the Peak District so it is still possible to see these hares as near as the general Sheffield area. In spring, with the snow gone, the white hares show up well and can be stalked for interesting photographs. I have always found them easier to approach than brown hares and I shall always remember a particular Irish hare on one side of a bunker in Dublin peering over the top at the distinguished mammalogist Dr Gordon Corbet peering over the other side.

The colours of the different hares are variable and as with all mammals it is interesting to note how they vary across their ranges. Mountain hares are generally greyer than the brown, but in Ireland (where there would be no confusion as the brown hare is absent) they are more red-brown. Most of our indigenous mammals are a shade of brown from the sandy

Figure 61 As the snow disappears, the mountain hare, still in winter pelage, shows up clearly against the hillside.

shades of common and pygmy shrews, beiges of wood mice and bats such as natterer's and horseshoes, grey-browns of hares and roe deer through to the yellows and red-browns of dormice, red squirrels and red deer. This reflects our late autumn, winter and spring colours when camouflage is most important. During the summer months there is so much cover that the pelage tones are not so vital. The white coat change in the mountain hare (like that of the stoat 'in ermine') has clear advantages when the animal is so exposed in the mountains.

As the heather grows in spring the hares moult out in the cover of rocks and heather clumps. This is when they can be most readily photographed and you can find their little dug tunnels: a habit developed one would guess due to the more exposed terrain where they live as compared with their lowland relatives which are content with such shallow forms in farmland.

# Red squirrel

During this century, since the introduction of grey squirrels, the indigenous red species has become confined largely to the uplands whilst the grey squirrel is our lowland species. This is dramatically illustrated by the distribution maps in Andrew Tittensor's published work on these species both in the *Handbook* and in the new Mammal Society booklet (see Further reading). Red squirrels survive in some lowland areas such as the flat, sandy districts of East Anglia around Thetford, but only where the acres of pines have provided an ideal habitat in an otherwise typical east England farming district.

The increase in fir plantations across the land will probably favour red squirrels again and they are certainly a challenge to the mammal watcher. You have to walk very quietly and listen for sounds of feeding; débris falling from the tree canopy is often your first clue to their presence. There are, of course, always those occasions when you surprise a squirrel on the ground under the pines and I have driven past red squirrels sitting on fence posts on the roadside in Thetford. The pale or 'white' tails are distinctive although introductions from Europe have been made and

Figure 62 A red squirrel in winter when the ear tufts grow as long again as the ear itself. Note the light tail typical of the British race, although all the colouring is very variable.

these have dark tails. The ear tufts are very noticeable in winter, as long again as the ears themselves. During these months you can watch right through the short day with prospects of success. The daytime feeding has dawn and dusk peaks, but it can be very frustrating craning your neck up with constant sweeps of the binoculars to watch the squirrels amongst the dense dark firs. The best pose to adopt when you locate a squirrel is to lie flat on your back, holding binoculars to your eyes and feeling the rising damp.

Even dreys are difficult to distinguish in the high treetops and my photographs of them have never shown much detail. In Brecon Forest and Snowdonia, where the two species overlap it is difficult to be certain which drey is which, but feeding sites are fairly easy to locate and it is

Figure 63 Squirrels take food to eat at particular sites such as this stump where a grey squirrel has eaten sweet chestnuts.

worth taking the reference books with you for identification of cone remains. Once you have found a good area you should stick to watching there because red squirrels tend to keep to the same places. In Ireland where the populations flourish in many areas survey and marking work is in progress with live trapping. I have never had such close contact with the species. If you take part in the work you may be allowed to handle them with very thick gloves. In areas where the populations of squirrels are large the damage done to conifers is quite dramatic as they strip the bark near the tops of the firs and eat the sap and soft layers of the tree underneath. In many cases gales break off the treetops as a result of this bark feeding.

Red squirrels are the only mammal species to have become extinct in my home county of Hertfordshire during my lifetime as has indeed happened in many other counties. It is upsetting to have lost such an interesting and attractive species, but we must always consider the trends in mammal populations. If red squirrels have declined on the basis of a natural population expansion/contraction we may see a return, especially with the growth of acreages under fir across the land. There have been booms and slumps in the past and our short lifespans simply glimpse a small part of the total success or failure of animal species.

# Grey squirrel

Grey squirrels are widespread and diurnal and therefore one of the most easily watched species of mammal. Often the first sound one hears in woodland is the scratching of claws on bark, or the swish of leaves as the squirrels move along branches. The intermittent clatter of seeds and nuts from the canopy will also reveal an otherwise silent animal.

I have heard red squirrels scream, but it is difficult to beat the grey squirrel for a range of chattering and churring noises. One screamed at me when I rescued it from a dog, bit through my glove and then chattered angrily at me from a tree for my trouble. The squirrels chase and argue noisily with these distinctive calls, but I have also been threatened by one, possibly on approach to a breeding drey.

The baiting area I use below a high seat attracts grey squirrels and they will stand clearly in view for some minutes if uncertain of you. It needs only a slight movement to send them away. If disturbed, but still confident, they will circle a tree, often at low heights as you try to see round to where they are hiding. In parks they become very tame and often attract as much interest in London Zoo, for example, as the carefully managed captive animals on show.

However abundant and damaging this introduced species may be, it is nonetheless fascinating to watch a relaxed grey squirrel running along branches, stopping to groom, hanging upside down to grip lower branches and then settling down to feed in a hazel canopy right next to your high seat. This is a demonstration of highly developed skills in a certain strata of habitat. Relaxed squirrels follow regular routes along the branches with attractive ease, but in a panic will go directly and more clumsily through the treetops. All this can be watched in good light and large field binoculars are an advantage in dense foliage as you can pick up your subject more easily if you lose it.

Figure 64 A grey squirrel feeding. Note the lack of ear tufts throughout the year and the white lines of hair up the tail. These squirrels may look very red on the flanks and legs in summer.

# Coypu

In Norfolk and Suffolk you can look for the coypu amongst the extensive reed beds and deep-sided, neglected dykes. Coypus escaped from fur farms in Norfolk in the 1930s and their burrows in the banks of the water courses caused obvious damage. The control of these aquatic mammals by the Ministry of Agriculture was launched at the start of the 1960s and was greatly aided by the severe 1962–3 winter which reduced their numbers considerably. Numbers have since recovered and their presence in parts of eastern Norfolk and Suffolk now looks assured. The arrival of the coypu and aspects of their feeding are well documented in Lever's book on naturalised animals (see Further reading).

My contact with the species has been confined to dead feral specimens and to watching captive specimens swimming with the typically low profile, nostrils clear of the surface, paddling steadily. I have skulls from dead specimens found in Norfolk and the large yellow incisors are very impressive. The molars are very close-set and angled outwards on each side.

Not much in the way of field observation has been recorded to date, although the damage caused to crops, especially sugar beet and some of the marshland flora, is known in detail. If you combine late evening birdwatching around the quiet waterways of their range in East Anglia, you can see the coypu moving out in water or onto farmland. Activity is usually confined to night time but they breed throughout the year and observations at nesting sites would be of interest.

Figure 65 The characteristic low profile of a coypu swimming.

# 6 Grazers and browsers

Although this chapter is largely devoted to watching deer, we will begin with red-necked wallabies, our only marsupial living free in Britain and then consider the breeds of ponies to be seen in the wild. Feral goats are also established in the mountainous areas of Britain and Ireland and these are discussed with white cattle and sheep at the end of the chapter.

## Red-necked wallaby

'Wallaby watching' has a good ring to it, even though it may seem a strange activity in the British Isles. However, as Grzimek shows in his *Animal Life Encyclopaedia* (see Further reading) this species has adapted surprisingly well to the harsh European winters, and, in fact, its introduction to our continent is not new; towards the end of the century it was possible to see these kangaroos (the family title) instead of deer on the meadows of the Rhineland and Silesia in Germany. (Out of the hundreds, if not thousands of releases and escapes which have occurred over the years, the feral species we are left with are those which took to the climate.) Derek Yalden has made a study of the wallabies in the Peak

Figure 66 Red-necked wallabies are distinctive in shape and active in daylight, but may be very shy.

District (see the *Handbook*) and Christopher Lever's book, *The Naturalized Animals of the British Isles* includes a detailed account of their presence both in the Midlands and in parts of the Sussex Weald. I believe at one time there were more of the sub-species of the red-necked wallaby in this country than in their home Tasmania, although there is another sub-species in north and west Australia and those introduced to New Zealand came to be estimated at half a million at one stage. I have enjoyed watching them on the hills of Whipsnade where they are a familiar sight, feeding with the Chinese water deer. Both species like long grass and scrub on the borders of open areas to retreat into for shelter and resting.

Cover is vital in the worst of the winter conditions, but even our most extreme weather has not wiped out the populations. There appears to be no fixed home area and in the *Handbook* Yalden gives heather as their main item of diet with bracken, bilberry, pine and grasses as other types of browsed and grazed food. A cautious stalk will give good views and although some individuals are very shy, others can be closely approached. There is an attractive symmetry to the shape and distribution of body weight for balance and the wallabies have the characteristic kangaroo hopping locomotion.

Their droppings are not left clumped as in most ruminants, but are more loosely scattered (see Yalden); I do not know of a published illustration of them. If you visit Whipsnade you can get to know the appearance of both the animals and their droppings which are always an important starting point for locating the wild mammals to watch.

# Horses

There are many opportunities to see semi-wild horses and ponies in Britain and Susan Gates has shown how interesting it can be to watch and study our free-ranging populations. She lists nine breeds native to Britain and Ireland: Shetland, Highland, Fell, Dales, Connemara, Welsh mountain, New Forest, Dartmoor and Exmoor. The origins and degree of direct descent of these breeds from the indigenous wild horses of the post-glacial period have not been determined but the Exmoor ponies show the most primitive features. Gates does not consider them a man-made 'breed' as such: the free-ranging ponies which form about seventeen per cent of the whole Exmoor population are neither wild nor domesticated and there may well be an unbroken line of descent from the original wild populations.

The pale colouring around the nose is a primitive feature and an erect mane is typical of the now extinct Russian and Polish tarpan. Grzimek gives a very good account of the breeds of horses in his *Animal Life Encyclopaedia* and interesting illustrations of their general behaviour accompany his text. Visits to eastern Europe or the Carmargue will give opportunities to watch local herds. In Britain I have enjoyed horse watching in association with deer watching on Exmoor and in the New Forest in particular.

To date, this has been a rather ignored aspect of large mammal watching and Gates has done much to encourage interest in it. She has shown how overlapping home ranges of the different pony herds can become exclusive territories as the young stallions mature together. (The home range is that part of a total environment available to an animal which is actually used by it.) Territories develop as groups or dominant individuals show aggression to others, sustaining their claims to areas by scent through urine or their faeces. Hence the advantages of latrine areas which concentrate scent at particularly important sites. The significance of dung piles in free-range pony herds is uncertain but the latrine habits certainly persist in all horse groups, wild and domestic. I live close to a group of horses which free-range ten acres of orchard and they use distinctive areas for defecation. There are occasional lapses, but concentrated areas are located in parts of the orchard which have remained unchanged for years. (In the same way, it has been observed that badgers competing for feeding areas will almost run from one dung pit to another to top up the dung and musk scent along their territorial boundaries each evening.)

## Deer

Deer watching is one of the most appealing of all mammal watching activities. As deer have been stalked in various ways as well as hunted since Man first developed these skills, there is much practical knowledge available on the subject, and the glossary of terms associated with their lives and behaviour is lengthy. A full list is given in F. J. T. Page's *Field Guide* (see Further reading) but we can consider a few commonly used names for aspects of their life cycle here.

Most male deer grow antlers annually and 'drop' or lose their previous set before the new pair grows in 'velvet' (living tissue which dies away and is rubbed off by the deer when the antler bone growth is complete).

Figure 67 The last strands of velvet hang from the fully grown palmated antlers of this dark fallow buck.

The antlers are used to fight other male deer in competition for females. Male deer can be 'stags' or 'bucks' depending upon the species, and the time of 'rut' or mating is usually at a particular season of the year. 'Roaring', 'barking' and holding 'rutting stands' are activities associated with mating; male deer will 'wallow' in mud to enhance scent, 'fray' young trees by thrashing their antlers against the branches to clean off velvet and 'scrape' at the ground to define their territory more clearly, particularly around frayed trees. Young deer are either 'calves' or 'fawns', and their mothers a 'hind' or 'doe' depending on the species, and the young are usually 'dropped' or born at the optimum time for food for the mother in the summer. Muntjac deer however breed continuously so that the winter fawns may spend the first weeks of their life in freezing temperatures when the ground cover is at its lowest. A Chinese water deer buck introduced to our unmated doe a month after the rut brought her into oestrous and she had the multiple birth of fawns usual in this species (three in this case) about a month later than the usual time of birth in the summer.

Different species of deer require different types of watching technique. Vehicles can be useful in many circumstances (see Chapter 2), but the standard approach to all deer is either to stalk on foot or sit in a high seat over well-used paths or feeding areas at dawn or dusk. However, the larger species tend to congregate in late summer and later still after the rut so that it can be better to appear initially like a casual pedestrian rather than a stalker. Walk quietly but boldly along a ride when you see a group of deer amongst the trees or on the edge of a feeding area and allow the deer to see you. They are probably already aware of you anyway, but keep walking; to stop would arouse suspicion and they would almost certainly move on.

Having located your deer, a slow consideration of the wind direction, best approach and ideal cover can be made when you are safely out of sight and scent. If you circle back with all conditions in your favour you should be able to watch the herd in peace. The true test of a deer watcher is to approach, observe and eventually leave without the deer having known they were being watched. As we will consider in the next chapter, this is also true of badger watching. So many people depart noisily, whether from hide or high seat, leaving a lingering sense of disturbance with the animals watched.

The more solitary, smaller species are best followed up in careful stalks which establish the routines of individual deer. Their behaviour follows the changing times of dusk and the first light of dawn closely through the year and feeding areas tend to be more specified than the larger more free-ranging deer in herd groups.

Our knowledge of deer and their biology is being extended by marking wild, caught individuals, taking measurements and then releasing them back into the wild. This involves people driving deer towards nets which, with luck, retain the animals long enough for other helpers

Figure 68 On a muntjac catch-up a strong nylon net on bamboo poles encircles dense cover. Deer are driven out, netted and boxed.

to rush up and handle them. As a result of such 'catch-ups' known individuals can be observed and studied so that the best management can be put into effect. The work is carried out at the point of capture or nearby so that release can be made as soon as possible. Work has been done in many parts of the world on marked animals and coloured collars are used to show individuals at a distance. Tattoos are also added for confirmation of previous capture at a later date when the collar may have been lost. To maintain the numbers and distribution of all deer such research and conservation activity is essential. Participation in catch-ups can be most instructive to a beginner and will also help field workers involved in deer study.

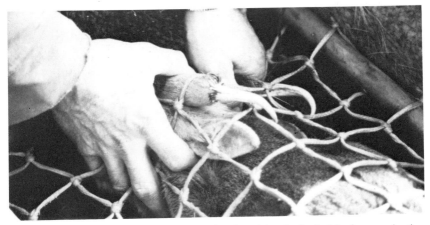

Figure 69 A muntjac buck (note the curved antler with a single tine) in the examination box. A tattoo is made in the ear and a collar fitted.

Catch-ups can however disturb deer considerably from an area. I discovered this recently when working with Dr Dansie on a muntjac catch-up. A buck and a doe were caught and collars fitted. Reports from around the village as the deer were seen showed that we had displaced the territory and it was four months before the doe was back in the same areas of cover as before. I am uncertain as yet as to whether the collarless

Figure 70 The weight of the deer is taken while it is in the box, a collar bolted on and the deer released back into its habitat.

buck in association with the doe was the same one that we had caught.

The life cycles of most of our deer are so clearly defined and the challenges of watching so varied that you can never exhaust your interest in watching these large, shy land mammals. The British Deer Society has published a series of booklets on the different species and both Dr Delap's *Red Deer* in this series and the new Mammal Society booklet by Brian Staines, *The Red Deer* (see Further reading) will give introductions to the biology and field signs.

In this section I have extended the muntjac material to include some observations made during my years keeping and watching this species in collaboration with Dr Oliver Dansie. There is a limited amount of information available on these deer, which justifies this extra space, but I principally wanted to demonstrate how observations can be collated over the years and put into graphs or tables to further our knowledge of mammals. Chapter 9 continues this theme.

## Red deer

Like the horses on Exmoor the red deer are great survivors. On the open hillside they are a challenge to the watcher, especially in areas where they are local and persecuted. Dr Peter Delap has taken some remarkable photographs in the Lake District during his thousands of hours of watching there. I am indebted to him for introducing me to these and to Lakeland roe deer in the snow, against the beautiful backdrop of the Pennines. Of all the books on red deer, the picture essays by Lea MacNally such as *Year of the Red Deer* (see Further reading) are perhaps the best works on Scottish red deer available and will tell the watcher more of what to look for than the less well illustrated accounts.

You must be prepared to practice very cautious stalking techniques with red deer and to crawl long distances if necessary. Try never to show a sudden head shape above rocks for example and keep checking carefully for individuals that are a little apart from the main herd and more on their guard. They will warn the herd the moment they become

Figure 71 Alert, young red stags sun themselves on the hillside in the Lake District. The antlers will become more complex and heavier until old age, ten or twelve years later.

suspicious. Where the open hillside gives way to forestry access, you will find the deer more relaxed as they enter the trees and, with the extra cover, easier to approach. In the deep, well wooded valleys of Exmoor I found approaches very different from the long, careful slog on the hillsides in the Scottish Highlands and much more akin to roe or fallow stalking. Tracking is very easy in the damp woodland and the red deer paths are clearly defined. In both areas, the telescope comes into its own for prolonged observation on an undisturbed herd or individual deer.

In Thetford, I have watched by the carrot fields on the edges of the

Figure 72 The defiant roar of the rutting red stag surrounded by his harem of hinds. The antlers are dressed with bracken and mud, the neck has thickened with a dark black mane and the under-hair is drenched in mud and semen.

Figure 74 A muntjac buck in velvet gives a warning stamp. Note its mobile ears.

forest and here you can see the deer in their true woodland environment, feeding out onto farmland. They are like the New Zealand red deer in this area, physically larger than the Scottish deer from introductions of Wapiti blood from North America. Many of our deer park red deer have Wapiti cross-bred origins, too and there is no better place to get to know the look of the deer species than the various parks which still manage deer herds. Richmond is an obvious site and I have been fortunate enough to spend many hours watching, photographing and tape-recording in Knebworth Park, Hertfordshire.

The roar of red stags in the rut is quite remarkable as I have described in Chapter 2. There is some debate about visiting deer parks in the rut when the most dramatic and fascinating events of the year take place as there is a real danger of disturbing the deer by over-attention and if this causes more aggression between the stags and reduces calving success, it

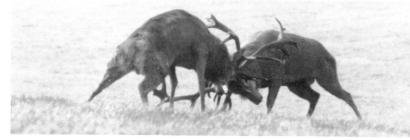

Figure 73 During the October rut two stags fight with powerful thrusts and noisily clashing antlers.

must be undesirable. However, with caution and restraint the deer watcher should not have an adverse effect and in the parks where the deer have to come into constant contact with the general public, their tolerance is considerable. Two of the best-known deer parks are Richmond, near London and Woburn in Bedfordshire. Local deer parks may be open to the public and it is worth enquiring if regular observations may be made. Some parks have several different species kept together. Red, sika and fallow deer will mix well and take up favourite areas of parkland.

The dominant, older red deer stags will try to round up and keep as many hinds as possible and the rivalry between stag harems causes the basic tension which makes the rut so theatrical and exciting. It is probable that the hinds select the stag they want to be serviced by rather than the stag being free to choose. There must be many intricate relationships between hinds themselves and with their large calves even as late as several years after birth. (They remain in with the same groups.) Old hinds always lead a group running across the park when disturbed or

Figure 75 A doe muntjac being approached by her nearly adult sized fawn.

Figure 76 A Chinese water deer fawn, one of a litter of three.

herded by Man. In the handling of red deer, such as during a catch–up, it is not the young stags one needs to watch, (the older stags are not handled), but the old hinds which can be surprisingly aggressive and inflict serious wounds with their hooves.

You must never disturb the hinds when they are calving in the summer around June. The date depends upon when copulation was successful during the three weeks or so of rut the previous September/October time. Sharp, early frosts are supposed to bring the rut on earlier and start the stags off sooner than a very mild autumn. One error regularly made by the public is to see a calf, or fawn in the case of other deer species, and think that because it is on its own it has been abandoned. The mother leaves the very young calf at hidden sites until it is following easily at heel. During this first period she visits the calf only to allow it to stand and feed. Never touch the young deer you may come across when out watching. The human scent may cause the mother to abandon it.

Park herds help you get to know your deer, but you cannot beat dawn and dusk watching of the wild herds, whether on moorland or in wooded valleys. My first approach to Scottish red deer entailed an absurd attempt to cross a valley and stalk over the brow of an apparently near hillside. Youthful ignorance of scale and distance found me exhausted from the rush and climb over a far greater distance than I had anticipated and as I peered over the final skyline (there always seems to be one more summit that you cannot see on approach), there were the deer gently moving on, almost as far away as when I had first seen them.

## Sika deer

Sika, which are found in a number of localities and deer parks now, make beautiful, eerie screams during the rut, quite distinctive from the red deer. Yet put very simply, they are red deer at the other end of their range, the eastern type, which freely hybridises with red deer when introduced into parts of Britain.

They are most frequently found in woodland and many deer watchers make an annual pilgrimage to watch the sika rut in the New Forest. They tend to keep to clearly defined areas and the typical deer signs of paths off main rides, wallows, fraying and droppings are easily located in the favoured areas. This is a particularly striking species and when watching old stag sika deer close to, amongst the trees in the poor dawn light, I have often felt I was looking at a primate face, almost gorilla–like in its dark glare from the grey, frowning forehead. They are very expressive also in the way they stretch and crane the neck to look at a detected watcher. In fear, they flare out the white hairs around the tail region in a very obvious way, high–step and slip away quickly, looking very dark amongst the firs.

Figure 77 A buck Chinese water deer barking in the rut in December. Note the long canines and thick, pale winter coat.

Sometimes the rut, which takes place from about the end of September to late October, is a quiet affair to start with and the calling is slow to get going. There is more of a territory basis to the stag activity, but does are fussed and rounded up in a similar way to the red deer. The stags scent the air as most deer and herbivores do with a characteristic raised nostril and air of rapt pleasure in the rut, known as 'flamel'.

The peak for calving is in June and sika are particularly attractive when juvenile. At this time, as with all our deer species except for the Chinese water deer, the antlers of the adult males (and females of reindeer) are growing in the annual cycle of loss and regrowth. In the sika the velvet tissue at this stage is very orange in colour, especially in the Formosan types. A very photogenic species altogether and fascinating to tape. On tape the parkland Manchurian type sika make a different sound from the more Japanese sika types of the New Forest and elsewhere when compared and it is well worth making recordings in different areas.

# Fallow deer

Fallow deer are most frequent in woodland and farmland and live very close to large urban areas. They are accessible to watchers in most parts of Britain and Ireland but have only local herds in northern Scotland. Most of our fallow deer have come from herds that have escaped or regularly enter and exit from the old deer parks across the land, but there are ancient herds in, for example, Epping Forest (now rather dispersed due to human pressure, particularly by the road traffic), the New Forest and Cannock Chase. There is great variety in the colours of these deer from white through spotted brown (menil) types to black.

Herds vary in size and can be just a small family group in areas where the deer are well dispersed and local. In places where they are used to the general public, the approach described earlier can be taken one step further and instead of walking along rides in camouflage clothing, bright, light clothing will suggest to the deer that you are just another tourist looking for somewhere to picnic. You can, in fact, take the whole noisy family and as long as the horde keeps moving, you can detach yourself, put your coat on and return to the location where you spotted the deer, wind blowing into your face, binoculars at the ready. Deer subject to much human pressure and poaching will associate the dark, lone, cautious figure with the men who stalk to shoot illegally or loose a gazehound.

Nick Myhill of the Forestry Commission told me of watching a doe and fawn fallow in long grass next to woodland. He had used the same sort of approach by passing the deer and then returning in the favourable direction. The fawn wandered towards where he had crawled for the final cautious approach. It detected him and was very nervous, giving the distinctive prance with stiff legs (see figure 78). Despite this warning to the doe, she ignored the fawn and resumed feeding after glancing

Figure 78 On detecting a human watcher, a young fallow doe prances away in a typical stiff-legged display.

towards the woodland. In a short time another doe appeared with a fawn and joined them. Clearly the doe identified the fawn's anxiety, but interpreted it as a result of the appearance of the two other deer. The group settled down to feed and the fawn took no more notice. Persistence and care while watching certainly pays off.

It is interesting to see how much more relaxed deer become at dusk and after dark. If you walk amongst deer at night they are more confident and treat you as far less of a threat. It is all a matter of being in their own environment at their most secure time, just as we are when in our own homes.

Tameness in animals is a study in itself and will vary from area to area depending upon their treatment by Man. A hand-reared deer released into a group of shyer deer reared by their parent doe will help calm the others down when they sense human presence. At the same time its tameness will be lost to an extent as a result of the caution and fear expressed by the other deer. So an exchange takes place and as something is gained, something is lost.

Dr Donald Chapman and his wife Norma who have contributed to mammal study in so many ways, have published a great deal on fallow deer. The best guide to the natural history of the species is their *The Fallow Deer* (1975) which extends the knowledge gained from the booklet guides published by the Deer Society. The rut can be as noisy as that of the red deer, but is usually based on the bucks defending a 'stand' of a tree or trees, to mate with does in this area. The bellow is more like a series of repeated belches. The time of rut will vary, but autumn is the peak and the bucks will round up does often in a frantic rush about their rutting stand.

All deer are expressive with their hooves and stamp and scrape a good deal. The fallow will turn over the mud and autumn leaf fall leaving scent and beaten bushes all round, just as the red deer and sika scrape up wallows and enhance their bodies with scent from an excellent mixture of urine, semen and water, all very irresistible to the does. Approaches to rutting stands should be made very carefully because it is easy to send away does you did not notice in cover nearby and so disturb the whole activity. All male deer can be aggressive and dangerous to incautious humans during the rut, especially the large species which herd.

# Roe deer

In contrast to the red, sika, fallow and muntjac deer which cast their antlers in the spring or early summer and regrow the new head during the summer months, the roe bucks lose their antlers in late autumn and the new set are ready for the midsummer rut, in July or August, just after the fawns have been born between April and July. This rapid mating after pregnancy is similar to that of the muntjac, although as will be seen later, fawns of this species may be born at any time of the year. Delayed implantation by the roe doe means that development of the fawn takes place mainly from the start of the new year.

As with muntjac and sika, the tail region fluffs up in alarm although there is no tail as such, apart from a small tuft of white hair in the doe. Their barks are more abrupt than muntjac, but I have never been tested on such a means of identification in areas where both species occur. When roe have barked at me they tend to repeat bark with larger gaps than the disturbed muntjac (see page 97).

Roe do not usually herd in the same way as the larger species discussed although they do congregate in good feeding areas and I have seen German photographs of large numbers together in snow. Distinct summer territories are established and prime watching sites are the courtship rings where bucks chase does around some kind of focus such as a bush.

Most roe watching is done either from a high seat or by slow stalking on foot. Richard Prior's books on roe stalking give essential information (see Further reading). The advantages of the high seat have already been discussed in Chapter 2, but although the risk of detection by scent has been removed and your identity is camouflaged behind the shape of the high seat, there are frustrations to sitting in one place when activity may be centred elsewhere. Sometimes it is more to one's temperament on a particular dawn or twilight to stalk slowly on foot. Keep to the general rule to walk a few paces, pause, raise binoculars, scan and repeat until contact is made. Many watchers claim that if you do not see the deer with the naked eye, you will not see it first with the field glasses, but as I said in Chapter 1 this repeated routine does slow your actions down. What the eye tends to catch is a clue to the shape of a deer. Something tells you that the pattern of branches or leaves is not quite right or you pick up the shape of a neck or a colour that makes you raise the binoculars. This then confirms the shape of a beautifully camouflaged deer.

Roe can be called with lures and my most successful use of the 'fawn lost' or 'fawn in danger' type of call was in Thetford during the early days of the summer rut. A few minutes earlier a buck had jumped out ahead, barking and stamping towards me for a few paces before going off with more barks. I found a rutting ring in the grass 100 metres ahead. Later I gave one squeak and was about to do a second (standing in long grass next to a wheat field on the edge of a pine plantation) when a doe came rushing up towards me.

She stopped 10 metres off as I raised my camera and then ran in a semi-circle to peer closely at me amongst the pines. I took a picture and she went off, reasonably satisfied there was no fawn in distress after all. It is exciting to have a wild deer running full tilt towards you, but at other times your lures can have no effect at all. Grass stems, the back of your hand – all kinds of calls can be made and tested as well as the manufactured ones.

There has recently been a gradual expansion of range of roe to old areas where they had become extinct and it is to be hoped that these small indigenous deer will be widespread again in future decades.

## Muntjac

I now come to the deer species I have kept for twelve years in our garden and watched for twenty years in the wild. Because of this bias it did seem to be the appropriate place to show how observations derived from watching in captivity as well as in the wild can be collated and used to fill gaps in our knowledge on a species still relatively little known. The observations are partly shown in chart form as anyone watching wildlife will find this a useful way of expressing their data in published form. All my work on muntjac has been shared with Dr Dansie, an authority on the subject.

Our species in Britain, Reeve's muntjac, has been present since the turn of the century and over the last thirty years a gradual expansion of its range from southern England to the Welsh borders and the south-west has taken place.

If you watch these deer regularly in the same habitats you will find that unless disturbed excessively they follow a routine which is remarkably predictable and quite different from the textbook view of 'very secretive' or 'difficult to observe'. They are, however, hard to photograph well because of their relatively small size and preference for areas of dense cover. Light is often too poor for a small deer picture and the exact routes from their retreats are not as predictable as those of badgers for example, so that flash photography is difficult.

The following subject headings are the kind of areas of study you can apply to any mammal you devote a great deal of time to watching. If you have filled your diary or notebook with descriptions of each visit to a site, you can best collate the material by writing such headings at the top of blank sheets of A4 paper. As each topic comes up as you go through your old diaries, turn to the appropriate sheet and add all the relevant data in numbered lines. This makes further summary onto charts very easy when all your diary notes have been listed.

## Habitats

Of all the sites where I have watched muntjac over the years, I have found that young fir plantations and woodland with dense ground cover are favoured, with overgrown, wild gardens, thickets adjoining farmland and neglected pits also popular. It was by regularly visiting three areas: an old estate with woodland and neglected fields, a young fir plantation and a blackthorn thicket adjoining arable land that I found how predictable the evening activity could be. Through winter and summer, the deer would feed out from cover following twilight with the same sort of pattern so well documented by Ernest Neal for badgers (see Further reading). Regular paths are used, but vary from evening to evening so that certainty of an exit from cover for instance, is not usually possible. Dr Dansie has carried out his research catch-ups in overgrown fir plantations in the main and I can recall very large concentrations of deer in some estates; as many as twelve deer have been caught at one site. Muntjac are frequently killed on the roads and use the same crossing places. They penetrate suburbs with regular routes and retreats, but at times are frightened, usually by dogs, into urban centres.

## Observed activity routines

When you visit a suitable site you will find that does move out of cover generally at dawn and dusk, with bucks following often some 10 metres behind, although sometimes several minutes may pass before the buck appears. This can give an appearance of solitary animals in each case, but it is remarkable how accurately the buck follows the line of the doe's trail. Even when close together, the buck tends not to divert unless disturbed: a doe once meandered across open grass in a semi-circle as I watched and then the buck appeared through the same gap in the fence the doe had used. He looked at the doe, but then pottered on, doing the same semicircle instead of directly joining her. In undisturbed areas, muntjac also feed in daytime and I have recorded this around noon in particular.

I have used a roe call to bring in muntjac, (bucks are particularly curious), and a small, plastic toy red London bus has just the right high-pitched squeak to lure the deer (and foxes). Try your local toy department.

## Sounds and displays

Our captive deer were given to us by Dr Dansie in 1969 and it has been possible to put together a summary of notes from diaries based largely on observations of them. We are lucky enough to have wild muntjac around the garden too, so that comparisons have been made between tame and wild deer behaviour. Our buck Jack gives a very plaintive squeak to a wild doe presumably in oestrous (on heat) even if she is out of sight several hundred metres away. If the scent drifts across on the breeze from cover, this is enough to attract the ever-willing Jack.

Muntjac are very vocal and are known as barking deer. As well as plaintive squeaks and barks, they click their teeth, squeak loudly, squeal and scream. I differentiate between these last two because the doe has an outraged reaction to an over-amorous buck that is quite distinct from the scream of a deer caught up. (Captive muntjac must never be kept with more than one mature buck because the doe in oestrous will be exhausted by too much attention. Does in labour may make a 'croak' sound with contractions.

Squeaking is associated with the fawns calling to their mother, but also with the attractive courtship runs and dashes which may follow regular circuits around trees and bushes. I have found a circuit in the wild and it was well trodden in the fashion of roe rings.

The scream can bring aid. I was once driving up from our house into woodland when I saw a buck nervously pacing across in my car head-lights. I drew up to watch and only then heard the screams of a second deer. I ran up a bank towards the area from which the calls were coming and found a doe trapped between fence posts. Judging by the path, she regularly squeezed through there, but heavily pregnant had now got stuck. I wrenched one post free and she ran on. I have had two other reports in my county of similar incidents where bucks had caught their antlers in fence wire and a tree root and the screams brought safe release.

Clicking is usually produced by bucks when anxious, but a doe has once also made this strange sound at me when I was close to her fawn. The sound is produced by a side to side movement of the jaws which may make the molars catch on gums or against each other in a grinding motion but no matter how hard I try, I cannot see exactly what our buck is doing to make the sound.

Barking can be a series of rapid, sharp barks on sudden disturbance, often associated with a bouncing stamp as the deer goes off stiff-legged, forcing out the bark as it lands on the ground each time. Or it can be a

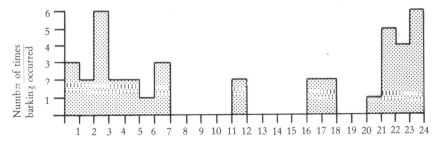

Figure 79 Here the frequency of muntjac barking at different times during the 24 hour period is shown, indicating the greater night activity. These results emerged from records taken from 1970–79.

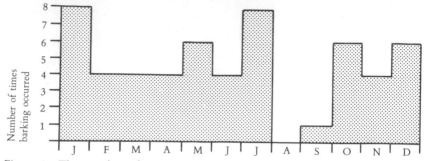

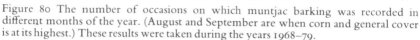

Figure 80 The number of occasions on which muntjac barking was recorded in different months of the year. (August and September are when corn and general cover is at its highest.) These results were taken during the years 1968–79.

regular bark given every four seconds or so for minutes on end. Phillip Kingsbury was counting barks on the edge of Ashridge and had got to about sixty-five when a door opened in a nearby house and the householder shouted 'shut up'. The deer instantly fell silent. (Our captive ones need a mouthful of peanuts to stop them.) Barking can be associated with the birth of fawns, but when I listed the records from over the years, they were fairly evenly spread and it is still a mystery why the deer bark at certain times and why others feeding nearby will not even look up but continue to graze despite the loud noise close at hand. Warning barks recorded were associated with Man, dog, cat and fox disturbance. One sure way to start our buck barking is to let a visitor's dog play with one of ours next to the pen. At night, cats will start off both buck and doe at times, especially when fawns are very young. Our buck has a higher pitched bark than all the does we have kept.

Stamping with the forelegs can also be audible in dry weather and is used as a threat. Both sexes stamp and even fawns will make a good attempt at this. Chinese water deer stamp, but may walk slowly whilst stamping the foreleg, more as a display walk. (A six-day-old muntjac fawn 'stamped' and a Chinese water deer fawn we reared used its forelegs to strike out forcefully when eagerly suckling at almost every feed as it matured. The muntjac fawns do not do this and it may be because Chinese water deer have multiple births and the fawns compete with each other during feeding as they mature.)

## Territorial behaviour

Muntjac have large scent glands on the face and appear to mark their home ranges by rubbing and fraying thin saplings on the sides of paths in particular. They mark each other (bucks frequently anoint the forehead glands against does) and after marking the saplings fray a thin slip of bark upwards with the lower incisors. Apart from footprints, these little fraying stocks are the first field signs you are likely to notice. Captive bucks and does love having their scent glands rubbed between

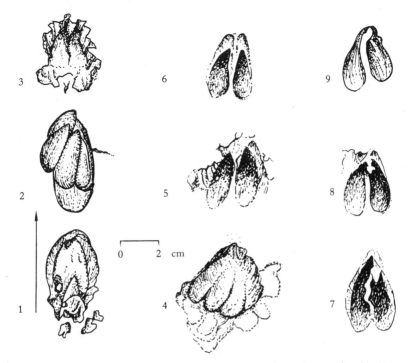

Figure 81 Deer tracks seldom look as simple as they do in the text books. Here are nine consecutive muntjac prints (about 25 cm apart) as they appeared in a line up a slope on sandy soil.

the ridged bones of the forehead and under the eyes.

Fraying can be applied to bushes as well as trees and is often associated with deep scraping and scratching at the soil with hooves. Interestingly, I noted that it was only after our captive buck, Jack, had started to fight with a wild buck which appeared at the fence, that he began to add deep scrapes to fraying stocks and parts of the fence line. On being given access to a new pen Jack made repeated routes to and from his established pen and merely frayed new trees almost at once (see figure 82). A new sapling pushed into the ground will receive immediate attention. The twist of bark at the top of the scratch is characteristic. (Deer have no upper incisors, just a hard pad of gum and bite marks on a young tree indicate rabbit or hare damage.)

Fighting involves interlocked antlers and the use of the canines to cut at the neck, (the skin is very thick in this region and wild deer frequently show cuts across the neck). Such attacks can be lethal to aggressors like dogs, but on the other hand large marauding dogs working in pairs have killed many muntjac locally in recent months. Does, heavy with young

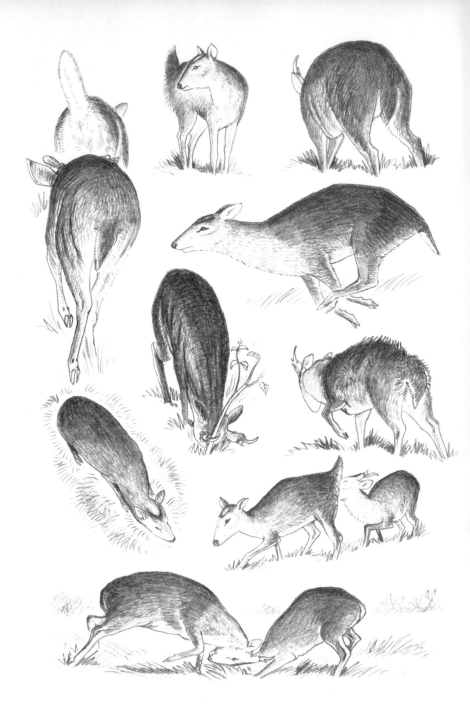

Figure 82 Muntjac behaviour. Top, left to right: tail raised in courtship chase (buck is active even in velvet); tail region very fluffed out in display to dog; normal relaxed tail when foraging; tail drops from upright at start of fright to be held down in panic; buck scent marking and fraying young stem; buck about to attack, head turning with back hairs raised and 'high-stepping'; doe in submissive flattened body posture; buck licking and pressing doe in oestrous prior to mounting; bucks fighting with antlers (canines also used).

are the most vulnerable, but are very courageous in defence of threatened fawns. The forelegs are used to kick and stamp an assailant. Rushes are made at the attacker as the deer fluffs up all the hairs in the tail region, which expands becoming very white and obvious with the ginger tail partly raised, and it arches its back holding its legs stiff and stilt-like. Hairs stand up on the lower back at times and the tail is held upright in mild anxiety, but in panic, the tail is held down as the deer runs at great speed for the nearest cover. Bucks spar with fawn bucks, but have little more than pushing games back and forth, head against head. Prior to actual fights with other rival bucks, the ears flatten back and down like those of frightened horses.

Our tame deer live in harmony with rats, but our buck killed a Chinese water deer buck in the same pen when excited over a doe in oestrous. (Despite the larger canine tooth, the Chinese water deer buck did not fight back. Doe Chinese water deer appear much more aggressive and put their ears forward, rush at others and may kick our fiercely with forelegs.)

The simple antlers are still very sharp and, being uncomplicated, only rarely become entangled with undergrowth. Complex tines would be a disadvantage in dense areas of thicket. Where visual contact is limited much use is made of scent to communicate. Bucks defend does in labour and pairs groom each other affectionately both in captivity and in the wild. They are very sensitive to the loss of a fawn and may show anxious behaviour including initial 'lost fawn' squeaks for some hours afterwards. Scent is very strong in urine and muntjac urinate for about fifteen seconds, sometimes longer, and defecate in regular latrine areas. Faeces usually scatter on impact with the ground, but sometimes remain intact and can be found on paths, possibly as added territorial marking. One complete scat includes about forty-five separate, dimpled pellets. Fresh heaps in latrines may number three or more with old ones at hand. I have found them in association with fox, badger and rabbit droppings in one small clearing.

Social rank in captivity is indicated by the dominant buck forcing a sibling buck to get up and vacate a site where the buck then lies down and also by first choice of feeding on the arrival of supplementary food. In certain circumstances does and bucks flatten their bodies against the ground on meeting each other. This is used as a sign of appeasement to a dominant animal, and has even been performed with a dead road casualty deer introduced to a pen. Strangely, I have once seen a young buck flatten to a fawn doe on the introduction of the fawn to his pen.

Figure 83 The doe muntjac (left) has a dark crown, whereas the buck grows long pedicles and short antlers, with ginger between the black 'V' on the forehead.

## Antlers

Despite the fact that muntjac does come into oestrous throughout the year, the bucks have antlers to a seasonal pattern and are fertile whether in hard antler or in velvet. In most deer the production of sperm is associated with the growth of the antlers to a stage when they can be used in fighting to hold rutting stands or groups of females against rivals. Our captive buck cast his antlers progressively later (see figure 84), with one exception, and with gradual increase in the length of antler as the pedicle length decreased, (see figure 85). One of our doe fawns kept by Dr Dansie developed small 'knobs' on the head where bucks normally grow the pedicles and even bled slightly from the top of the growth, (22nd July 1977). In the same year a wild and a captive buck shed antlers in late May (23rd and 25th May) whereas our old captive buck retained his for another week.

## Feeding

In the wild I have frequently watched muntjac grazing on grass and it is common to see them browsing on bramble along the edge of dense thickets. The close access of cover is clearly also important for security: they step nervously and jerkily across open areas especially if suspicious of an observer. A wide variety of foods is listed for the species and muntjac are no trouble to feed in captivity, unlike Chinese water deer which prefer grass. The only other foods water deer readily enjoy seem to be brassica leaves such as cabbage, cauliflower or broccoli. The staple artificial diet of our captive muntjac is now a dog food:

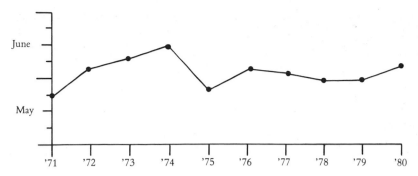

Figure 84 The dates of antler drop by one muntjac buck from 1971–80. The 1975 drop was caused by a fight with a wild buck when one antler was pulled off on the wire of a fence; the other antler was cast the following day.

the dry mixture Valu-mix manufactured by Gilbertson and Page (see Appendix III). Grass and general browse is taken in the pen and the autumn apple fall is a valuable additional food. A hand-reared Chinese water deer has a taste for Valu-mix and the others sometimes eat chicken feed, but general vegetables are ignored by this species in captivity.

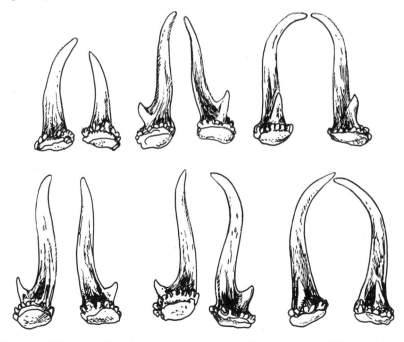

Figure 85 The antler development of the same buck muntjac; top left, 1971 (second set) to bottom right, 1976.

Figure 86 Hand-reared fawns should be regularly bottle fed with powdered milk substitute from farm suppliers. Stimulation to feed and defecate is essential either by use of a damp disposable cloth or, as here, by a volunteer foster mother.

## Breeding

Courtship chases and mating begin as soon as the previous fawn has been born and the doe may be pregnant again within a day or two. Copulation usually takes only three to five seconds and the buck thrusts the doe forward, but the preliminaries to mounting can be prolonged involving much chasing and licking of the doe by the buck. I have watched our buck chasing a young doe at eight months old when her first oestrous may have commenced, but mating was not observed. The

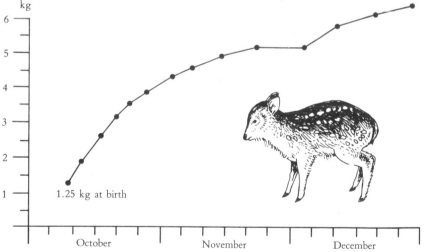

Figure 87 The growth rate of a male muntjac fawn born on 8th October and measured until late December.

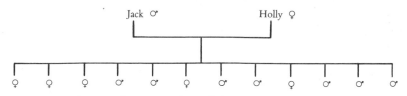

Figure 88 Here the sex of successive fawns born to one muntjac pair is shown from left to right. Twelve fawns were born in seven years and the doe died in labour with the last, a large buck fawn.

doe only looks heavily pregnant in the last week or so before the fawn is born, seven months after mating. Fawns weigh about 1.5 kg at birth and the development of one over nearly three months is shown in figure 87.

It is important with hand-reared fawns to have a dog to lick the faeces and urine away from the fawn, a function performed by the doe in the wild. One picked up in January 1975 had been fed on condensed milk for a week and when given to us was gummed up and almost unable to feed, but our dog quickly cleaned the fawn and kept the digestion flowing thereafter. Fawns should be reared on dried Lambs' Milk Replacer or sows' milk substitute. In a few weeks they jump about and 'dance' with excitement, doing mock courtship figure of eight rushes and using trees as a focus for games. At three months, buck fawns can show mounting and juvenile mating behaviour: a stiff-legged, crouched walk with tail up and penis erect was typical of a young buck just weaned. Head twitching is a feature of fawn play but is retained by adults, and the bucks will flick the head sideways in preliminaries and when disturbing the doe from rest to pursue her in courtship chases.

The sex of fawns born to one of our does was five does to seven bucks: (see figure 88) and she died in labour with the last, a large, buck fawn. She had the twelve fawns in seven years. Figure 89 shows how fawns

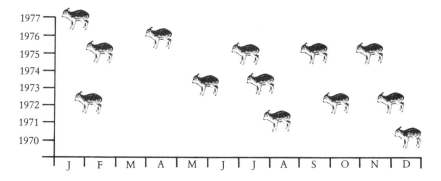

Figure 89 The births of muntjac fawns born between 1970 and 1977 in the Welwyn district of Hertfordshire are recorded here; note the distribution throughout the year.

may be born in any month of the year. Winter fawns are less likely to survive fox and dog predation when the cover is very low. The mortality of captive fawns is not high despite low temperatures; ours would sit in snow and freezing night temperatures without ill effects. At first our doe kept the fawn in cover, visiting it to feed, and it was only after several days that she had the fawn following at heel and took it into a warmer straw-lined shed with her.

I hope these additional notes on one species will show something of the way in which watching can give useful data to build up a picture of the life history of an animal. What the charts cannot convey however, is the many hours of watching pleasure in wild places and in the garden pen, or the hours of work my wife Anna has spent rearing fawns, feeding deer and recording many of the observations. These basic areas of study are just as applicable to other species such as badgers. A full study of muntjac has still to be written. Eileen Soper produced a delightful book in 1969 *Muntjac* and as mentioned previously, the Deer Society booklets are very good for all the deer species except our next subject which has not yet been covered.

## Chinese water deer

Although established in the wild between 1939 and 1945 from introductions at Woburn Park earlier this century, Chinese water deer have a much more limited range in Britain. They have bred successfully when introduced to extensive reed bed areas such as Woodwalton Fen, Cambridgeshire and may be watched in the general farming areas around Whipsnade and in Woburn, Bedfordshire. They are also found in parts of adjoining counties. In a deer survey I took part in along with about 300 other watchers on Ashridge, southwest Hertfordshire in 1972, the day's count produced: 168 fallow, 30 muntjac, 9 foxes and 2 weasels, but only one Chinese water deer. They favour the grassland borders, but do move into the thicket areas of mixed deciduous woodland.

The fawns are born in May and June and large litters can occur although this is not usually the case. In five does I was able to watch with young at heel at the farm site, four had single fawns and one had four. Both our own does have had litters of three of which one survived in the first and two in the second. Unlike muntjac, Chinese water deer do not breed continuously; they do however have the added interest of these multiple births. They are delightful to watch in grassland, their heads giving the impression of three black buttons on a yellow face, the nose and the two eyes peering at you from the long grass. They have large mobile ears.

Chinese water deer populations do seem to suffer during hare shoots on farms and I was told by a regular participant in these drives that they are easily shot because they tend to try to hide in the ditches. Their method of escape is usually that of retreating into deep grass cover. It is incredible how they can hide behind virtually a single clump of cocksfoot grass, shrinking into themselves when they detect danger and lying up. On walking past I have found that they do not easily detect a person who is stationary and camouflaged, although they will pick up any movement.

It is interesting that this small deer, with no antlers, but long canines in the buck, should have a distinct rutting time. This occurs in the second half of December and the deer congregate at the Whipsnade farm in impressive numbers. The bucks and does have a hare-like gambol as they chase round. The bark is a distinctive 'no', almost a yelp, with about four to six second gaps as in muntjac. It is linked to alarm; I once frightened one which barked repeatedly and then set another one off some 100 metres away in the dark. There is also a very attractive warble or whistle at this time which I have only once heard out of rut. Chinese water deer are a much shyer and more difficult species to keep in captivity than muntjac. They panic easily and need cover to hide behind throughout the year. All deer become more relaxed as cover increases in the summer.

Chinese water deer feed at dawn and dusk, but as with muntjac they have a small midday feeding time and I have frequently observed midnight feeding. They scream in extreme distress. Although the books say that the canine is long in both sexes, in the buck it is much longer, over two centimetres, whereas the doe canine only just shows below the upper lip against a dark patch of hair.

As young deer mature they become difficult to distinguish from adults. The yearling Chinese water deer have a more chubby look initially and are slighter in the body. The shape of head and neck is less refined. They are also less cautious than the mature deer. (In most of the larger deer species, the head length is worthy of note: it is generally not as long as that of the adult and the nose is blunter, even when the body size seems identical.)

Although I have had as many as thirty-three Chinese water deer in view at once in the rut, at other times of the year they are generally solitary or loosely aggregated and very secretive. The courtship with its bouncing runs reminds me of rabbit or hare groups courting. Four may run about together and the does do look as if they prompt certain bucks to keep interested when pursuit flags. The bucks approach does head down, necks stretched out. Closely resembling roe deer these deer are a beautiful species to watch and there are considerable gaps in our knowledge of them.

## Reindeer

Reindeer were once distributed throughout Britain, but finally became extinct in Scotland, having survived longest in the northern habitats, about the ninth or twelfth century. In Scandinavia reindeer have been herded by the Lapps for a thousand years and most are semi-wild animals.

Reindeer eat lichens, grasses and some plants. Both sexes carry antlers and the species was successfully re-introduced to Scotland in the early 1950s. The Reindeer Council carried out this work and the herd was largely managed by the late Mikel Utsi. I got to know Mr Utsi and the work of the Council through the Deer Society. The herd is well worth a visit if you are in the Ben More Forest Park area of the Cairngorms.

Figure 94 Reindeer cows are the only female deer to carry antlers, but these are much slighter than those of the bulls.

The distinct click of the large hooves is a surprising sound on your first encounter with these deer. When I first drew one Mr Utsi was quick to point out that they have a bulbous nose instead of the more typical rather pointed, angular deer nose. The deer are herded to keep them in the best feeding areas throughout the year and will move to the high ground in summer to avoid the large insect populations of the valleys.

## White cattle

When I first saw a group of the ancient white cattle I was surprised at how solid and almost blunt their features are and how different they look from the modern breeds. They are the last surviving descendants of the prehistoric wild white cattle and the most famous herd is at Chillingham, near Berwick-upon-Tweed.

If you are visiting the Farne Islands to see the seals, Chillingham is close at hand and the public can be shown the herd on a guided tour from 1st April to 31st October. If this all sounds a little academic to the mammal watcher, I still reommmend the observation of these find herd animals. The squared-off, muscular head has a mass of curls on the forehead and

Figure 95 Chillingham ancient white cattle; a herd enclosed and isolated for over 800 years.

the distinctive features are black (or dark brown as at Chillingham) inner ears, nose and ring around the eyes.

There has always been a risk of disease to the herds and they have nearly died out at different times in the past. As well as Chillingham Park, the herds at Cadzow Park in Lanarkshire and Chartley Park in Stafford-shire are ancient survivors and small herds have been established in some other parts of Britain. This lessens the danger from foot-and-mouth disease which might mean that a whole herd has to be destroyed during an outbreak.

The bulls fight for herd dominance very much in the manner of red deer, and should be treated with caution. It is interesting that the most famous work our greatest wood engraver, Thomas Bewick, produced in Newcastle was of a Chillingham bull and one of the best-known etchings of Charles Tunnicliffe is of a bull with cattle overlooking the Cheshire Plain.

# Feral goats and sheep

Feral herds of goats live in many parts of upland Britain and Europe. The wild ibex types of Spain, Central Europe and southern Europe south into Greece are adapted to mountain terrain and show great skill in the way they scale the screes and narrow rock shelves.

I saw my first herd of feral goats when climbing in Snowdonia. They appeared small with very loose, shaggy coats which shook as they jumped down from ledge to ledge in a very deep stream cutting with a total disregard for the damp rocks and depth of the gully. The herd was in the foothills of Chnicht overlooking the Snowdon range, but the goats also move into the remote high terrain, too, feeding on the rough grazing beyond most sheep penetration.

The upland areas are regularly visited by hill walkers and climbers so that camouflage clothing is both irrelevant and dangerous in such areas. The goats are so used to seeing the bright, fluorescent colours necessary for safety in the mountains that watching in this clothing causes little concern. On Tryfan a group of us climbed past a feeding herd without any disturbance to the grazing animals.

The rut is in late summer and autumn and the kids are dropped in early spring. It may prove more economic to manage the goats in favour of sheep in years to come due to the value of skins and meat. They eat more bracken than sheep and being more adapted to very exposed areas can give a better return to those farming in such places.

The Soay sheep of St Kilda are now a familiar parkland species and show how the ancient sheep looked before breeding gave heavy bodies and thick wool. There is a November rut and lambs are born the following April. I have watched these sheep for several years alongside the deer in Knebworth Park and although they are an attractive animal, dark brown with fine horns, I cannot say that they ever distracted me seriously from the endless fascination of deer watching. This is a breed to care for and promote however.

Figure 96 Soay sheep are the most primitive type of sheep in Europe. Horns are present in both sexes, but those of the ram (left) are much heavier. The ewe's summer coat is moulting out.

With all these browsing and grazing animals we have considered, it is the challenge of stalking and watching the wild ones which really captures the interest. Parks will show close-up details, but will not test your skills of field craft and you cannot substitute the atmosphere of watching in our wild places.

# 7 Predators

It goes without saying that predatory mammals are exciting to watch. We have all seen the well described and often beautifully filmed scenes of life and death in the East African plains showing how dramatic these events can be. A description of a simple routine act of predation will however, illustrate the rewards of careful observation in almost any type of habitat. This is an event which occurs millions of times a day across the world – a predator taking its prey.

'A scream came from the pit to my right. I had circled the badger set and as I hurried to look over the pit edge an adult rabbit ran past with a hesitant sort of lope. In the pit a younger rabbit was struggling with a stoat locked onto its neck. The stoat had bitten it across the left side of the back of the neck with one ear pinned down, the other free. As the rabbit struggled the stoat clung on, its body apparently relaxed.

'The struggles became death throes and when the body became still, the stoat let its grip go and looked around. This is the time when many meals are lost to other predators including Man due to the familiar rabbit scream which immediately draws attention to what has happened. The stoat dragged the rabbit by the neck to a nearby burrow, but after a few seconds reappeared to look round again. I had stepped closer and froze as it looked out, thinking there must be a nest of young stoats there. I was wrong. The rabbit was dragged out by the neck and taken across to a hedge.

'I stalked carefully behind on the leaf litter as they reached a gap in the branches. The rabbit got stuck and the stoat began to hurry exerting itself to get the burden moving again. It was like a poacher getting caught up on a fence in his haste to get out of a private wood. Then it was across the bridleway with the rabbit and lost in the long grass of the adjoining field.'

## Stoat and weasel

The above account from my diary described the first time I had witnessed an actual kill, although I have watched stoats stalking rabbits and heard kills being made many times. Stoats tend to be unpredictable predators, but when a female is feeding juveniles, habitual visits are made to good feeding areas such as rabbit warrens. Presumably the fact that it is easier to carry juvenile rabbits back to its nest of young makes a warren the ideal summer site for views of diurnal hunting and retrieval.

Figure 97 Note the whiskers on the foreleg of this alert weasel.

Weasels have a habit of appearing suddenly and going on their way equally quickly. I confirmed their love of following boundary lines, whether hedgerow or wall, when Longworth trapping for voles. There is nothing like the smell of recently caught voles in the traps to tempt a weasel inside. I caught two on the line of a hedge in a short time in this way. You know at once if a weasel is inside your trap and young stoats make even more commotion. If they have fallen asleep, the powerful scent should warn you. At home, we have kept a weasel rescued as an abandoned juvenile. Tom, as he is known, shares our living room for recreation and I could fill a book with all his activities. What is most marked is the speed, agility and climbing activities of the species. Not that this isn't obvious when you watch them hunting. The most prolonged views I have enjoyed have been when waiting quietly in hedgerows when weasels have appeared working their way along the paths next to me. They can pass by without noticing the observer and movement seems to catch their attention much more than the obvious

Figure 98 A stoat about to retrieve a dead rat. The black end section of the tail is longer in proportion to the body than that of the weasel.

human scent.

It is much easier to follow the hunting techniques of stoats from a high seat, than to pick out the smaller weasels, mostly hidden by cover. The persistent hunting by the scent, vision, scent routine and the culminating stages of the kill are dramatic. Rabbits really can freeze with fear at the final moments which is hardly surprising. The much quoted reaction of the famous explorer David Livingstone on being mauled by a lion gives a good description of the sense of paralysis or, more accurately, anaesthetic experienced in such events. Livingstone felt no pain, fright or fear of death, but just became limp and lifeless. This saved his life, because the mauling stopped and he recovered to tell the tale. P. H. Beard's book *The End of the Game* describes the event in detail (see Further reading).

Probably the best advice for regular stoat and weasel observation is to keep to a regular beat yourself and wait until you come across individuals. If you note the time and place carefully and survey the surroundings for runs, you may establish contact on a regular basis, particularly as I found if the animal is an adult female feeding young in the summer. Your reaction on confrontation with these small carnivores should be to freeze at once and remain still. Keepers frequently exploit the reluctance of the animals to run away on such occasions by waiting until the temporarily surprised animal reappears and resumes its activity. It is a pity that these animals are controlled, because they keep rabbits down very effectively. Litter after litter of juvenile rabbits was taken from the warren in woodland near my home as the mother stoat fed them to her young. There is evidence that the effect these predators have on game rearing is negligible although on occasions it can look serious in a concentrated area of game bird nests. It has been said that a summer thunderstorm can do more damage in a day to partridge chick numbers than all the local predators can in a year. But keepers have 200 years of practice behind their views and I have more worries about the countryside without the estates and keepers than with them. So much valuable habitat is left to our wildlife as a by-product of game conservancy.

Perhaps the answer is a payment scheme whereby landowners are compensated for all the predators which can be proved (say by a local independent member of the County Trust for Nature Conservation) to have bred on a keeper's beat. Once keepers are caring for buzzards, sparrowhawks, badgers and so forth, our countryside will be enriched. Payments would offset any losses to game and visits by a local Trust official for example would not affect the coverts or rearing programmes.

# Pine marten

The careful stalk does much to give you the advantage over a hunting mammal. Listen for the alarm calls of small birds which are a good guide to the presence of a predator of some kind. Regular watching in one area may accustom the very experienced watcher to different reactions, but I cannot say that I have been able to split those of weasel and stoat. I found in Co. Clare, south-west Ireland (where there is only the stoat or fox to confuse with the pine marten moving through cover in daytime) that one had to listen for a more prolonged threat. Stoats and weasels move more quickly through cover whereas pine martens feed and circuit their territories more slowly in daytime and largely on the ground.

I discovered this when shown all the pine marten pathways through the lush woodland undergrowth of west Ireland. I had always imagined these beautiful mammals spending their time chasing through the branches of trees after squirrels and retiring to hollow trees. Although they do climb freely, eat squirrels and often breed quite high up in ivy clad old trees, their main diet consists of earthworms, beetles and ivy berries taken at ground level. Only in parts of Europe are red squirrels recorded as the main food item.

Pine marten paths are clearly defined amongst the ground flora and often take in boulders and fallen trees where droppings can be found. Scratch marks on trees and fresh dens amongst roots and boulders are signs of activity. Sightings can be made in daylight, but are most likely at dawn and dusk, and the tip given me was to stalk along the main rides.

I was able to watch the martens in close-up in the captive colonies although these tended to be nocturnal. It is the combination of their coat colour, facial structure, thick tails and dark legs which make them so appealing. I did not hear any sounds from the wild martens even though I slept two nights in the Irish study area, but the captive animals have a distinctive call and the threatening growl is quite remarkable. Unlike the ubiquitous stoat and weasel, the pine marten range in Britain is very restricted and it is a mistake to think you have to watch such rarities to be a mammal watcher. The few people who have studied these animals in detail are expert in field work and familiar with the remote habitats where they mostly survive. Some do come into gardens and feed from bird-tables. It would indeed be fascinating to see them re-established across Britain and this would contribute to the control of grey squirrels. In Europe the beech marten is typical of the more deciduous southern woodlands and this species also uses regular pathways on the ground. The ranges of the two species overlap on the continent.

## Polecat and ferret

Pine martens and polecats are not easy to watch. Even with knowledge of their dens and regular visits to their habitats, I have never really 'watched' them as such, and glimpses or brief encounters cannot compare with regular observation. Night binoculars are an obvious aid, but these carnivores are small and fast moving. However I have kept both polecats and polecat-ferrets and found them highly entertaining as well as instructive in large outdoor runs. Polecats have a considerable variety of whickering, threat and courtship calls and our captive animals are often reminiscent of miniature otters in their play. The wild polecats survive and are extending their range from Wales into the bordering

English counties.

Polecats tend to be strictly nocturnal, but I did encounter one once crossing a Forestry Commission track near Brecon in daytime. The area is well used by polecats and their runs contour the hillside in close association with the badger paths. I have found dens, or at least holes smelling of polecat musk in rabbit burrows and at the base of rock outcrops. If you have a chance to stay in polecat and marten country, I can

Figure 99 The head of the male polecat (left) is much thicker than that of the female (right). The eyes appear to be open even when they are closed due to the white patch over the eyelid.

only suggest patient watching and long waits based on the local knowledge of people who work or study there. With respect for both the animals and the people who have helped you find the best sites, you may be lucky. All the radio and tracking techniques used on badgers (see below) are now applied to these species so we will know more and more about their elusive life cycles as time goes on.

There is considerable debate about the extent of interbreeding between polecats and ferrets. Ken Walton's views (see the *Handbook*) are based on the most detailed study of the species that I know and he has found remarkable consistency in the skins of polecats from Wales. He has noted the increased occurrence of white throat flares or white paws on the borders of the range, where the species is extending into England. Escapes are by no means rare and polecats often come into captivity to put some 'wild' blood into someone's stock and as often as not escape again. In the main range, the external features of escapes of mixed blood seem to be quickly absorbed into the wild population which breeds true in a few litters. On the perimeter of the range, where the population is smaller, the traces of escaped ferrets or polecat-ferret crosses show up more frequently.

Figure 100 A family party of polecat and polecat-ferret crosses.

What I notice most about the wild caught polecats from central Wales is not the blackness of the hair, but the dark chocolate brown tinge which makes the black hair and cream underfur seem much darker overall than that of a cross-bred animal. The facial pattern is often discussed, but the feature I have found most consistent is the side band of dark fur which in my experience never goes below the mouth in the recently crossed polecat-ferrets, however dark they may look, and is most marked in the summer coat.

I would certainly recommend anyone interested in carnivores to keep ferrets, if space allows, because this is the small, working and tamed descendant of the wild polecat, (probably southern European in origin), that Man has tamed for his own use.

If you keep and work ferrets for rabbits, there is a choice of detectors available to use in the location of your animal underground. Many ferreters do not like them because anything put as a collar around the neck may catch on roots. However, if this does happen you know exactly where the ferret is. Apart from not losing your ferret, one great value of the detector is to be able to follow (very quietly, with soft steps of course) the progress of the predator underground. If you have been waiting and watching quietly and think that the ferret is holding on to a rabbit, you can turn the detector on and find out its position by variations in the volume of the transmitted sound. If it is still exploring, you will trace its journey through the burrows and can leave it to do its work. All this is also possible with polecats, although mine move much more quickly than ferrets.

I have found as a result of using a detector that rabbit warrens are much more complex than I had expected and than external features may suggest. It is surprising how far they penetrate underground. Following the animal around all the branches of tunnels below brings you to little entrances, obscured by leaves perhaps or hidden behind fallen branches where that cheerful, enquiring face appears, perhaps 15 or 20 metres away from where you entered it. More likely still a rabbit will have bolted from this forgotten hole.

The quiet, skilful routine of ferreting is not only instructive for the mammal enthusiast. It is the ideal way to manage the rabbits, for example, on nature reserves. They must be controlled by law and it is our duty to keep our reserves as well managed sites which do not affect the farming and forestry work which goes on around. Because there is no need to involve shooting or gassing, ferreting creates no disturbance or danger to other species present on the land.

We must always try to manage our wildlife, where it is essential, in the most humane way possible. Ferreting is so like the natural predator/prey method of rabbit control that polecats, stoats or weasels practice every day in the wild. The only difference is that we net the holes and catch the rabbit which otherwise may have escaped. You will learn a great deal about predator behaviour from this interest and you can usually find a local ferreter who is prepared to take you out initially. If you are really interested join the Ferret Society (see Appendix III) and get practical experience before you finally commit yourself to owning a ferret.

# Fox

When you see a fox close-to, the fine features, colour and above all the movement of the animal attract the eye. It is not surprising that people who love horses and live in the countryside so often spend their lives at the hard work of foxhunting. On this controversial issue I am always on the side of the fox despite the damage it can cause in certain circumstances, and it is sad that so many hands are against these beautiful animals.

These days one form of control does not prevent others: foxes are trapped and shot as well as hunted, but survive surprisingly well. In its favour, foxhunting has given us many woodland coverts and preserved wild places where farming might otherwise have dominated an entire area. There is no doubt that in some places management of foxes is necessary and if a humane shot at close range is not possible, I would rather hunting continued and the snare be made illegal. There is certainly no alternative to the Fell packs and their working terriers. The hounds are followed on foot and the management of hill foxes to reduce losses of lambs is felt to be essential by hill farmers. On this theme, dogs are no help when watching mammals and dogs out of control in the countryside cause enormous damage to farm stock and wildlife annually. They can however provide some very exciting views of mammals which would otherwise go unobserved. My terriers have often put foxes out of thickets and provided me with beautiful close-up views. Foxes can be so confident and casual in these circumstances. It is also instructive to see the reaction of the wild animals when under a certain amount of pressure.

On the day I wrote these notes, I took the dogs for a walk close to home and they got onto a scent in a thicket where foxes live within metres of free-range hens. I heard a sound nearby as the dogs chased through the thicket and a fox went past a metre or so inside. Then another followed it and in a few minutes one fox came out and stared at me. It decided not to break past and went in again. There was no sense of panic. It slipped over the brambles and low branches like a cat. The other fox came out too and seemed to be running right up when it stopped and looked carefully at me, 10 metres away. It turned and slipped silently into the cover again. Its mouth was not even open and there was no sign of the mildest exertion. The dogs, on the other hand, returned, tongues lolling and excited.

Watching at earths can very easily frighten foxes off. They are restricted to a breeding site between March and July, but have alternative sites to move cubs to. Baiting the area keeps them interested and I have found that food put down regularly at a badger set is shared by foxes as well as birds, squirrels, and small mammals. I have even used a product called Fox Lure which was originally made to encourage foxes to stay in coverts for hunting. It is basically aniseed and fennel mixed with lemon in a dark paste and like Draw Game in liquid form. It is available from Young's of Misterton (see Appendix III). When using it in an artificial earth I had made, both badgers and foxes (and one of my dogs) quickly came to explore the hole and even seemed to eat the Fox Lure so that, hung in a bag from a branch, it may add to the success of your baiting area.

I have often caused barking by foxes when watching at earths, especially when a vixen has detected me and is calling to the cubs still at the entrance. It all makes you feel very much an intruder, but there are few more atmospheric calls of the wild than fox screams and barks.

Even under pressure foxes maintain their cat-like delicacy and precision of motion. On a catch-up for deer I watched a fox run past me from cover and stop at the net. It ran down the outside of the netted area but wanted to reach the apparent security of its usual haunts in dense bramble cover. It bobbed along the net with none of the panic which entangles the deer as they rush into the light mesh. The tail flowed behind in perfect balance with the undulating body as it pushed and pulled back to avoid becoming caught up. It is a different matter if a dog is in hot pursuit however, when sudden haste can cause them to rush the net and become entangled too.

My longest views of foxes in the wild have been of those feeding in grassland at dawn. Overgrown pasture with tussocks of cocksfoot is a great attraction, particularly in wintery conditions. As cover dies back and the grass is less and less thick, the field voles are concentrated into smaller areas, and the lightly covered runs become increasingly insecure. The foxes sniff out and spot the voles with precise pounces. Through binoculars they look magnificent hunting like this in the dawn sunlight against frosty grass.

The older reference books largely ignore two important aspects of fox biology. The main diet of small rodents and earthworms and the surface living behaviour away from the breeding season should be remembered when watching for the species. Reference books like the *Handbook* will give you details of diet and breeding times.

Recent work with light intensifiers at night has shown that foxes will follow badgers to favoured areas of pasture to feed on earthworms. These and small rodents, tend to be the staple diet in many areas and interesting feeding experiments by David MacDonald have shown how field voles, bank voles and wood mice are favoured in that order. Food storage as caches buried for later detection are important as larder provisions for nights when food is hard to find. You will, therefore, find foxes feeding more often in field areas and on field edges than in the centre of woodland. Hill and mountain foxes present greater problems of observation but the location of active dens followed up by watching can produce good results. In summer, the activities of foxes will continue after first light and when I think back to my most rewarding times of watching, hot sunsets in summer and dawns in autumn and winter provided the best watching away from the breeding earths.

Breeding can extend over several months, but the matings at the beginning of the year give peak births around late February and early March for views of the cubs round the earth in May and June. It all seems to pass so quickly and the cubs grow rapidly. 'There will always be tomorrow' tends to be a mistaken philosophy with fox watching because so many disturbances can frighten the animals and so many hands are against them that 'your' cubs may be gassed or dug out. It is best to keep quiet about them if an earth has public access.

Figure 101 Fox cubs, their ears alert, have worn the soil bare around the earth as they mature.

Cubs are weaned in six weeks and are fed at the earth before they leave to explore extensively, although they quickly scatter around an earth as they mature. Dawn watching can give some delightful views of the large cubs playing and hunting round the hedgerows, increasingly independent of the earth. The strong fox scent and food débris when cubs are still being fed at the earth is unmistakable. The first thing you notice when a fox has been around your area is the characteristic scent. This is particularly obvious in damp weather and fox urine marks a section of path very distinctly. Foxes will use earths to escape into and I have frequently found them in our local badger set after the hunt has been through. Much of the year they will sit up in dense cover rather than retire underground. Where there is little surface cover, dens of all types will be used as retreats.

It can be confusing for the watcher when a fox is using a badger set and the same tunnels. Usually the foxes exit earlier in the evening in such circumstances. Badgers will use the same parts of the set despite the strong smell of fox and it alarms me that gassing may take place where fox evidence remains after they have moved, but where badgers are still living. Badgers rarely take food back to their sets because the sow continues lactating after the cubs have been emerging regularly at dusk and are foraging nightly around their sets. By the time they are weaned they are already familiar with the best areas to catch earthworms and may already be digging out rabbit, rat and vole nests on their own.

So for foxes, baiting an area regularly, watching at the breeding earths and stalking at dawn particularly in favoured open areas will bring the best views. In urban areas you may be able to see foxes feeding in gardens.

The phenomenon of foxes and even deer colonising suburban areas is comparatively recent but perhaps not so surprising when we consider how Man seems bent on covering the entire surface of the world with urban sprawl.

Scent and sound, our familiar points of detection are important in fox watching although those I have frightened on encounter have usually seen my movements. The greatest number of foxes I have watched in one evening (apart from litters of cubs) is five adults leaving an area in the same direction from dense forestry to feed out in fields. Each moved along the edge of young firs and one was distinctly older and thinner than the others. On another night at the same site a doe muntjac chased one of the foxes out of the dense cover around the firs only moments after it had confidently trotted into the area. Deer will defend their young with great courage and I have even heard of people being threatened by a muntjac doe, our smallest deer species, when a dog passed close to a fawn by a footpath. Foxes will however, take fawns when the opportunity arises and their hairs can be found in fox faeces.

One of the most detailed accounts of fox watching I know of is by Roger Burrows in *Wild Fox* (see Further reading). In talks I have often quoted the reasoning behind his notes on why foxes may kill all the chickens in a run. People frequently use the derogatory observation against predators that they kill for the sake of it without needing any more than one bird for example. It is our action in concentrating their prey items in artificially high numbers in one place which sets the scene for such an event. (I speak as owner of twenty-six free-range chickens at last count.) If protection is inadequate and a fox gains entry, the frightened birds flapping their wings will trigger the predatory impulse until all such signals have ceased. Hence the 'blood-lust' accusation.

## Badger

Badger watching is remarkably rewarding and however many times you wait quietly by a set, once you have been caught by the watching bug, there is a sense of excitement and achievement every time a black-and-white face appears and with a cautious scenting of the air, the animal emerges from the tunnel entrance.

Dusk has always seemed the most successful time for watching at sets; my dawn visits to see the badgers return have been less productive and one tends to be distracted into fox watching as the first light of day spreads across the sky. Not that it matters very much. The great thing is to be out when most people are in bed.

If you are quiet and have kept to the rules, a pair of badgers (and often

Figure 102 Watching silently and still at dusk, down wind from a badger set. If conditions are right, badgers may nose out, scent the air and emerge.

more with the cubs of the year) will appear as if on a stage in front of you. In many places large spoil heaps outside a set can build up over years of use to look just like a little theatre set. The animals disperse as time goes on, but you could not get a much happier combination of an appealing and large mammal with, as a rule, its reluctance to rush off when first active in the evening.

I find it more difficult to write about badgers, even with the inspiration of a large badger set near my home, than about any other species. Yet I have watched badgers for over twenty years now and have spent more time in their study than on any other mammal, apart from deer which live with us anyway. So much has been written about the species, from the unique and highly successful *The Badger* by Ernest Neal to what seems to be an endless flow of other books as if everyone who has spent any time watching badgers feels they must rush into print.

So we had better consider badger watching in practical terms and pass over most of the marvellous evenings out at sets. Endless anecdotes will not provide you with watching skills. Sets, which are often such impressive structures in their own right, mean that our subjects are limited to one area for their first appearance. The rules are fairly simple, but we must stick to them for consistent success and it is often when we are overconfident that we spoil watching.

Scent is vitally important and it is always necessary to consider this, with particular reference to local eddies and changes of direction which can so often occur in woodland and on the slopes of hills where badgers prefer to site their sets. Wind can swirl round pit edges and it is essential to check at the last moment that your scent is not being carried towards the set entrances at the site where you want to wait.

You can stand against a tree although it is less strenuous if you sit or lean against a wide trunk, feet resting comfortably at right angles to your body. Keep your body exactly in line with the tree because any new shape on either side will be noticed if it juts out into a normally clear patch of sky. Alternatively, sit on an inflatable cushion against a bush or behind cover where you can look through leaves and branches. At nature reserves or similar sites a high seat is ideal. Sitting on leaf litter, even in dry conditions, is not to be recommended.

As a general rule, follow twilight and try to get to the set about half an hour before dusk. February can be cold, but watching this early can be as instructive as in the spring when the cubs are above ground. Dr Neal's first book (see above) is a classic in style which transformed interest in and treatment of badgers. His second book *Badgers* (1977) brings all the information up to date because so much has been added to our knowledge

Figure 104 A characteristic pounce on a small mammal by an adult fox, hunting in lush summer ground cover.

of the species in the intervening thirty years. Both books inspire you to go out and watch, but here are a few words of advice.

Do respect the peaceful set these animals have established for themselves. Think of a total stranger tramping into your front room and sitting down to watch you come down to breakfast. Each time you scratch your chin, the interloper's binoculars will follow every movement. If you get fed up and hide under the table, the stranger may cough loudly, get up and crash out through the front window. Not very pleasant.

Arrive early at a set and leave only when the badgers have moved off or are unlikely to be frightened. Do not relieve yourself on their main path as alien scent could deter the badgers from their own territory, or talk noisily to a friend as you depart. If you are taking pictures, do not disrupt the whole evening with repeated flashes as each animal attempts to emerge. Use fast duration modern electronic flashguns which are less disturbing to the badgers. They are an amazingly tolerant and resilient species, but there is growing pressure from watchers at sets and humans always seem to put their own interests first.

You may not see any badgers at all after two to three hours at an obviously occupied set. This is a familiar occurrence to regular watchers, but only recently has research work with infra-red binoculars and marked badgers shown why this happens. Badgers have been observed out feeding and sleeping under a convenient hedgerow without returning to the set and then feeding again for an hour or so. Alternatively in very good feeding conditions when earthworms are abundant on the surface, a marked animal may sleep on in the set and not bother to emerge the following evening until quite late. In August they may sleep out in the maturing corn and not be back at the set when you are there.

The harsher the conditions, particularly in droughts, the longer the badgers will need to feed and the earlier they are likely to come out. You may get better views but delays caused by human disturbance at such times are even more undesirable. I saw a cub regularly feeding out in daylight during the dry summer of 1975 and conditions were even more extreme the following year.

In the poor evening light, until you see your first badger or badgers, the set entrances and the area surrounding them trick the eyes and take on the appearance of black-and-white badger faces as dusk merges into dark. If there are a lot of badgers at the set you may see several together and a rush of bodies round the holes, but often just the one nervous face sniffing the night air from the security of the entrance will be your first encounter. Relaxed badgers scratch and you can make good use of this

Figure 106 A large, dominant boar badger on a spoil heap outside the typically bare set entrance.

by scratching at your clothes to emulate the sound when nervous badgers are uncertain as to whether to emerge fully or not. It seems to tell them that if another badger is already out, all must be safe.

Once you have seen how the badgers are behaving you can adapt your watching to the conditions. If you plan to watch and photograph at a set, my advice would be to observe carefully at a distance initially and only move in closely when you have seen how the occupants are behaving. When you get to this stage, keep your disturbance to a

Figure 107 Badger cubs have a fluffy look and the black stripe is pale around the eyes down to the nose tip.

minimum. I prefer to leave my arrival at the set until as late as possible to reduce the chances of scent if I want to take photographs close to entrances. A very strong breeze, steady rather than intermittent is the best type for keeping your scent away from the animals.

Recently, with a picture in mind for this book, I visited my local set late and stood behind an oak four metres away with the breeze from the set entrance coming at me quite strongly. As the set is only 500 metres from our garden it is easy to leave raisins a little earlier in the evening and know that human scent will be virtually gone by the time the badgers emerge. If I am too early, a carrion crow usually takes them. Raisins are a useful bait for badgers because they blend in with the background in pictures, tend to concentrate the family round an entrance as they hunt each one out and provide a good nutritious food, safe for cubs. I planned to stay only for two quick pictures and then leave because conditions had been dry. I arrived at 9.15 and suspect that the boar had already gone because I did not see him at all and he is usually the first out and away. A fox slipped past above the set, just a silhouette against the skyline. In ten minutes two cubs emerged. This was my first view of the new family and as always it was an exciting moment. I took a picture as the cubs snuffled out raisins. It was their first experience of the flashgun and they grunted with surprise and rushed into the hole, only to reappear thirty seconds later with the sow. They all fed round the entrance and I managed to take a second picture of the sow with one of the cubs. They again went into the entrance and I slipped away quietly, half an hour after my arrival.

If you want more light to watch by, a red filter on your torch can be less disturbing than a white one, but do experiment. At some sites you will find badgers nervous even if a red paper filter has been taped over the torch beam; at others the occupants tolerate red light, but not white and yet others ignore any light, even from flash photography. The location of a set is definitely an important factor in successful photography. Where a set is close to a road, headlights flash past regularly, broken up by foliage so that the occupants become accustomed to this. At other sets where this does not happen, remote even from distant house lights and where Man may have persecuted the inhabitants you may find the badgers highly nervous.

Badgers' field signs are so obvious that the observer can quickly pick up paths, crossing points on roads, hair tufts on barbed wire and dung pits. Badgers will repeatedly use dung pit areas, especially where different colonies are competing for territory.

Intra-specific reaction (the behaviour of one species with another) is more likely to be seen at sets because foxes and rabbits for example tend to favour the same sites. Whilst rabbits frequently use set entrances, I have found that badgers enlarge and use rabbit burrows frequently and foxes freely share entrances with badgers. I have seen a fox emerge rather later than usual and rather faster, too, due to the badger following. Iain Watson, watching in Scotland, told me of a weasel at a set which went too close to a foraging badger. The badger struck it with its paw and the anger expressed by the unfortunate smaller animal had to be heard to be believed.

Badger watching holds a curious enchantment, that of being in the presence of large, attractive mammals so totally independent of Man, yet always threatened by him. It will reward the time and effort you spend on it – despite the insect bites, cramp and rheumatism!

# Otter and mink

Otters have declined across most of their range in Britain in the last twenty-five years for a variety of reasons such as pressure on waterways, pollution, water extraction and hunting. This has been well documented and publicised, and the tragic demise of the otter therefore presents even greater problems for the would-be otter watcher. A rare, privately published account of the Culmstock Otterhounds that I came across revealed that the number of otters killed annually up to the second half of the 1950s averaged approximately twenty with many more hunted. Before otter hunting became illegal, to try to understand the psychology behind it and the behaviour of the otter under pressure, I attended two hunts by the Culmstock and the Bucks and Courteney Tracy Otter-hounds during the late 1960s and early 1970s. It was depressing to see the hunts find such little trace of otters in the once very favourable Devon and Somerset country and on the old Ouse waters. Ironically one hunt follower complained to me that the master was now so worried about the otter's declining numbers that if the hounds picked up an otter's scent, he would take them off in the other direction in the hopes of finding a mink for them to kill.

Otters hunt by night and may be on the move for ten hours before resting up in the morning. If hunting with hounds commences in the otter's territory it may be disturbed at once and I have seen an otter mask with 'hunted for eight hours' proudly engraved underneath. This would mean the animal was under pressure for food initially and then from pursuit for a total of some *eighteen* hours. This is far from humane and I have never seen the need for management of this useful and highly intelligent predator. Local control around trout farms for example should be by fencing, not destruction.

I have seen otters in Scotland and tracked them in Co. Clare, Devon and on the Essex coast, but have never seen the species in my own county of Hertfordshire. As recorder for my local Natural History Society for the past twelve years, I have received about one report a year from the rivers in our area, including the occasional breeding record, but inland counties such as Hertfordshire must rely largely on a surplus of otters from the bordering counties and even the traditionally good coastal counties in the east have very few otters now. The dramatic decline of the species in lowland Britain and across much of Europe is now attributed to chemical pollution of rivers and streams, particularly by farm chemicals. Research is still in progress on this important subject, but it does appear that the otter is at the end of a deadly food chain and no rapid recovery is likely until our waterways are made less toxic.

Figure 108 A wild otter seen off the west coast of Scotland swimming to land with a crab. Many otters drown, trapped in lobster pots.

If you want to watch otters with relative certainty, you must go to the remote northern coastal areas such as the west coast of the Highlands or better still, the coasts around the Hebrides and Shetlands. The otters in these sites are much more numerous than at any inland sites (the density is approximately one per kilometre), and they appear more tolerant of observers in daytime. Their activity may be related more to the tides and less strictly to the dawn, dusk and night hunting we associate with river-based otters. Otters pick up movement very quickly and you should keep very still on sighting one. On one occasion the slight dip of my binoculars caused an otter 50 metres offshore to vanish so effectively that I did not see it again.

Figure 109 An otter spraint on a river bank showing the mucus or 'jelly' and the inconspicuous nature of the faeces.

Once otter presence is known and fresh signs including the spraints, which encourage the growth of bright green algae, and small deposits of anal jelly (important in fixing the scent used in territory markings), are found you can commence vigils for the actual animals. Ian Coghill has given a very interesting account of 256 otter resting sites observed over twenty years hunting in the Borders and Severn tributaries. Most resting places were in the roots of ash trees on the water's edge and were associated with deep water sections of the river. The majority of these overhung the water and it is this type of tree which the water authorities like to 'tidy' up and remove. Stick heaps both man-made and natural drift were favoured next and those partly submerged in water were preferred. Again, water authorities remove these. Rock holts including dry stone construction, railway bridge bases and finally the many types of drain or culvert retreat were also listed

Otters also lie up in 'couches' (as do badgers in secluded areas) such as in reed beds, amongst willows, in forestry plantations, rough grass and hedgerow, up to 50 metres from the water's edge. A few unusual sites have been recorded including three (only) in badger sets, some in rabbit holes and one under the driver's seat in a Morris 1000 – the otter swam out of the window.

Clearly, the best way of encouraging the species would be to allow more natural resting sites. Breeding holts are probably less of a problem because by their very nature they are secretive places, but the fewer resting sites you allow your species of mammal, the greater the pressure it will be under. What struck me about the rivers in the west of Ireland where otters are still to be found, was the beauty of their natural banks and the cover left alongside the water. Even the river through Ennis has old fallen trees alongside. No tidy, suburban minds at work there.

Philip Wayre describes many aspects of the otter life cycle in his recent *Private Life of the Otter* (1979). Captive breeding for release into the wild is fraught with problems, but a very worthwhile aim. His Otter Trust which promotes this is based in Suffolk and visitors are welcome (see Appendix III).

C. J. Harris amassed a great deal of information in his book on otters of the world: *Otters* (1968); it is a book to refer to rather than read from start to finish. Other useful titles are Elaine Hurrell's *Watch for the Otter* (1963) and the recent Mammal Society booklet *Otter Spraint Analysis* (undated) by Jean Webb.

I have not heard of the reactions between mink (established from mink farm escapes over the last thirty years) and the indigenous otters by any observers. Valuable work is however now being done on this subject.

I have seen mink on a river in Hertfordshire, but my best views were of one hunting regularly along saltings on the east coast which was to be seen each morning at first light and on other occasions at dusk. The effect of the mink on the water voles was dramatic. They swam out from each bank of a cut and came towards me like a miniature armada before escaping to safer ground.

In this area the otters never seemed to use the same waters although at least one was present further along the coast. All wild mink seem to look black and the colour varieties of mink farms seem to breed out in a short time on escape.

# Wild cat

I have to admit here that I have not seen a wild cat in the wild. There are many beautiful specimens to be seen in captivity, but on my five or six stays in Scotland I have not yet been successful in seeing an actual hill cat. I look forward to a glimpse one day, for with this species, that is all the watcher tends to get.

Long stays or actually living in the territory where wild cats survive can bring results and a Scottish friend tells me the hair colour varies from area to area so that you can tell more northerly specimens from southern ones. The large, ringed and blunt-ended tail is a good guide to distinguish the species from the domestic tabby gone wild. It is physically larger and the body stripes go over the body rather than longways down the fur. There is a dorsal black stripe but this does not extend into the tail. As with polecats and ferrets, wild cats can interbreed with domestic breeds. Kolb, in the *Handbook* gives interesting figures for hybridisations

Figure 110 A Scottish wild cat. This photograph was taken in captivity; the cat was caught as a kitten swimming in a Wester Ross sea loch by Gavin Maxwell.

from Suminski's list of colour and cranial characteristics (1962): the Scottish wild cat was estimated at 66% pure whereas European types averaged 63%; the highest degree of purity was from Poland (73%) and the lowest from the Swiss and French Alps (44%).

The rarity of the species and the typically remote mountainous habitats it frequents are the result of long persecution by keepers on the grouse moors which continues today in places. A gradual spread outward from its range is to be hoped for and this appears to have commenced southwards, across the Scottish border into England.

The activity of the wild cat follows very much the same dawn and dusk pattern of so many predators and deer. Millais found it was unusual even for the Scottish stalkers and people working in wild cat areas to see them. All his years' experience produced only one description of a cat stalking a rabbit (and this was provided by an aquaintance) where the rabbit became as distressed as those hunted by stoats in the final stages of pursuit.

Largely due to persecution our wild predators have become very shy as well as local in distribution. Watching them will always be difficult and the conditions often trying, but their intelligence and beauty is ample reward for our efforts.

# 8 Marine mammals

There is something very special about aquatic mammals. Their movements in water and the very association of these animals with beautiful river, estuary, coastal and sea habitats adds a special appeal for the watcher. Unfortunately, the remoteness of these habitats and the difficulties of watching mammals in water, or in waterside places has kept these animals in a similar category to bats. Such mammals are easily neglected because they are difficult to study and unless you make the effort to visit the wild coasts, or live overlooking the sea, you will not get to know whales or find the inspiration to look them up in the books which show how amazing their biology is.

## Whales

The term 'whales' (or the cetaceans) covers the great whales such as the blue, fin and right whales, lesser whales such as the pygmy sperm, white and narwhales, dolphins and porpoises: all are whales in the general use of the term. Despite the difficulties just mentioned there are now regular whale watching boat trips out from the Californian coast, for example, to see the great whales on migration. These are the greys and in places the humpbacks, which can be heard on recordings, calling with their incredible voices through miles of sea. Over-attention by watchers is causing concern that the whales are being disturbed and this is always a danger as tourism takes over from individual watching, although the growing interest in whales is very encouraging.

In Britain and Europe much is being done to promote a better understanding of whales through recent books and Mammal Society publications. Peter Evans has produced an excellent, low priced guide (see Further reading) and has allowed me to base figure 111 of whale sightings on his published maps, painstakingly collated from available data.

If you are able to holiday or live by the coast for extended periods your chances of seeing whales from the shore are much improved. In the late summer, presumably when porpoises are following the seasonal movements of fish, a friend who lives on the west coast has seen schools from his home overlooking the sea as many as three times in one week. Evans describes large movements in spring and late summer which suggests genuine migrations, as he says, probably offshore-inshore. Typical school sizes are of less than ten animals, but odd records go up to a hundred or more.

Sites particularly worthy of mention for whale watching across the

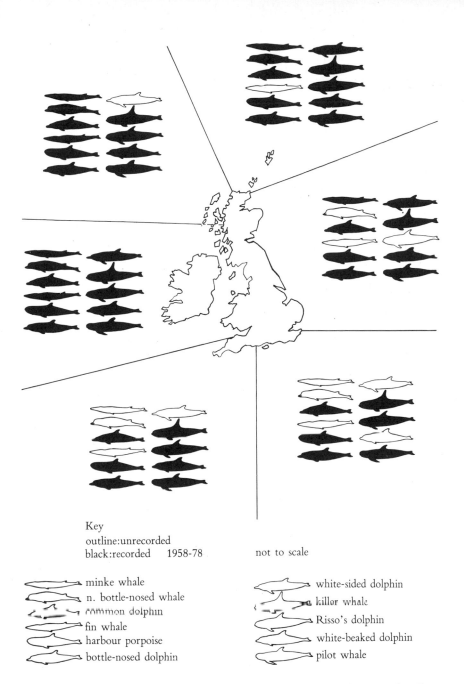

Key
outline:unrecorded
black:recorded    1958-78    not to scale

minke whale
n. bottle-nosed whale
common dolphin
fin whale
harbour porpoise
bottle-nosed dolphin

white-sided dolphin
killer whale
Risso's dolphin
white-beaked dolphin
pilot whale

Figure 111 The geographical distribution of 11 cetaceans in British waters, based on material in Evans, 1980.

world are off the west coast of North America and Canada (grey whales in particular), Hawaii (humpbacks); the east coast of North America and Canada (humpbacks) and Norway (humpbacks and fin whales). Japanese and Soviet coastlines have a considerable variety of species and hunting is continued here and from floating factory ships in the North Pacific and in parts of the southern hemisphere. Whaling is also continued off the Peruvian, Chilean and Brazilian coasts of South America, all on major migration routes. There are two excellent wallcharts available produced by the *National Geographic Magazine* which show the great whales and their distribution on a worldwide basis.

The destruction of our whale populations is well publicised and tragic when one considers that substitutes can be found for whale products. The conservation of our dwindling stocks of whales is a complex subject and well discussed by Bonner (see Further reading). Even with total protection, the changes Man has made by intensive fishing have altered the fauna of the sea so that the food may no longer be available to the whales. In addition, when the whales were reduced other species expanded and now the competition for food may be too great. Bonner does not see a recovery in the numbers such as the early whalers witnessed in the foreseeable future, even with total protection.

In European waters we do not boast such advanced whale watching as is now found on the west coast of North America or Hawaii, but a variety of cetacea occur across the north Atlantic. Some twenty-two species have been recorded in British waters and the British Museum (Natural History) has a very good wallchart of these species.

From Peter Evans' material in *Mammal Review* (1980) it is obvious that the harbour porpoise is the most numerous whale about our shores with over 12,000 sightings listed since records began. White-sided, white-beaked and common dolphins come next. Bottle-nosed dolphins are fairly frequent. These are the most typical species kept in captivity

Figure 112 The action of the tail muscles and flukes of cetaceans, such as these common dolphins, propels them powerfully through the water.

and I can thoroughly recommend going to Dolphinaria to see them close to; Risso's dolphin, long-finned pilot whales and killer whales (exceptionally handsome and also a success in captivity) are recorded in some numbers. Occasional sightings have been made of euphrosyne dolphins and of a number of whales: minke, sei, fin, humpback, right, pygmy sperm, sperm, northern bottle-nosed, Cuvier's, beaked species, white and narwhal.

Whale watching is most feasible from a ship and if you have an opportunity to go on a cruise you are more likely to be able to see dolphins and the great whales. The blow hole on the top of the head in cetacea gives a distinct spout (when air is breathed out and condenses as it cools) so that it is possible to identify some species from this, (see figure 113). It is best to familiarise yourself with the characteristics of the different whales by reference to the books available. *Wake of the Whale* by K. Brower (1979) has some exceptional pictures by William Curtsinger whose work has also featured in the *National Geographic Magazine*.

Humpbacks look grotesque in some illustrations, yet seen in their element they have great beauty and grace. Most of the great whales have baleen plates or slats instead of teeth to strain their plankton or in some cases small fish food. The water is expelled as the mouth is closed and the food swallowed. The sperm whale is the largest toothed cetacean and lives on squid, cuttle-fish and various other fish species. The migration routes, along parts of which the great whales are often watched, follow the ocean currents between feeding grounds and the warmer waters where they have their young and court one another. It is remarkable to think of them suckling young in the water and breathing air even though their diving can be over a mile deep with periods of an hour between spouts.

Whales are warm-blooded, intelligent and communicate well. The dolphins and porpoises use echolocation through water to navigate. (Their spouts are not usually visible and do not aid identification.) The more primitive river dolphins which may live only in fresh water in some places have very simple eyes relying on echolocation to find food and each other. Some are blind and the sensitive snout aids the detection of food in muddy rivers and estuary waters.

Whales are regularly stranded on our shores, even up our larger river estuaries, and any opportunity to see these animals at first hand should be taken up. I do recommend the study of these mammals even though opportunities to watch them are rare for many of us. As I have already indicated their biology is just as fascinating and complex as that of bats. I feel a link between the two because, put very simply, one order of mammals evolved to suit an aquatic existence and the other an aerial one. Both ventures presented particular problems and the ways in which they were solved make their study all the more fascinating. See Appendix III for details of the recording scheme for cetaceans seen in British waters.

| humpback | bowhead | right | sperm |
| --- | --- | --- | --- |

| blue | fin | sei | Bryde's |
| --- | --- | --- | --- |

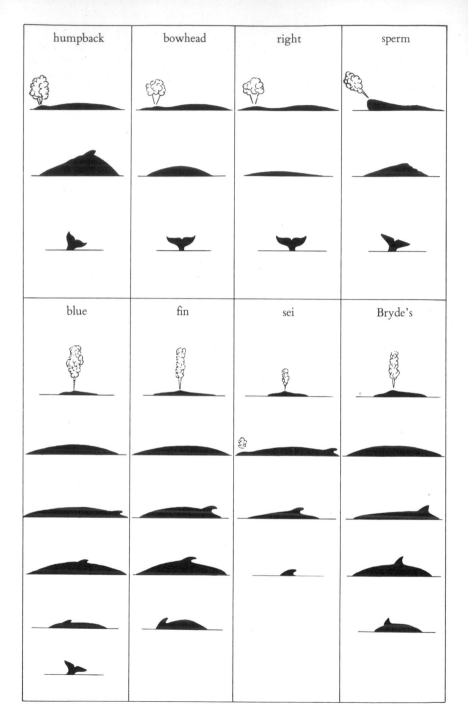

# Common and grey seal

The common and grey seals breed off our shores and there are occasional vagrants. The ringed, harp, hooded and bearded seals are rare visitors and need special trips to arctic waters for most of us, but the common and grey are very well distributed around the European coastline.

Away from the main breeding areas, seals may be encountered throughout the year. Many people fail to notice these individuals however and the following account of one of my own sightings illustrates this.

I had been fishing for bass on a south Devon storm beach all day as the tide turned and came in. A misty rain had alternated with a damp haze. A few people had walked past on the cliffs and across the beach, but only now with a brightness to the sky and a watery sun perhaps twenty people were scattered around the remaining sand. Suddenly a head seemed to bob about in the white foam. I raised my binoculars and found a grey seal had arrived unobtrusively near the centre of the beach. I withdrew my fishing line at once and watched for reappearances. It swam about looking around the cove. At this stage I looked to see what interest it had caused, but not one person had seen it. I was down on the rocky water's edge with the sea breaking all round, but even with the large seal between me and the people on the beach, nobody took any notice. I watched with pleasure as the seal, one of the most interesting and largest of British mammals, appeared and disappeared. It finally vanished out of the cove across from me and nobody was any the wiser.

Seals are best watched from land during their breeding times and when they haul out during moulting. My best views have been off the Pembroke coast of southwest Wales. For grey seals October is the peak month for seeing the pups, cows and bulls, although they are a month later on the Farne Islands and December is the peak for Scroby Sands on the Norfolk coast. Around April there are also seals hauling out for moulting.

Common seals breed in the summer with peaks from mid-June to mid-July. I have enjoyed my closest views of adults and pups not in the main areas such as the Wash, but off the Essex marshes. The greatest care should always be taken when cows have pups because disturbance can cause distress. On making a landing with our Jack Russell terriers at a site where I had tracked an otter and fox in the mud between tides, two adult seals and a pup moved off and were seen by the dogs. The dogs went prancing along the marsh edge and the cow swam away with her pup along the cutting in the marsh. The bull remained and watched the dogs closely some 20 metres offshore. It then bobbed and every so often splashed noisily at them with its head in threat.

I called the dogs away and left the seals in peace. We had watched the

Figure 113 Blow patterns and swimming and diving characteristics of the great whales (after Leatherwood, Caldwell, Winn, NOAA Seattle 1976).

Figure 114 Common seals hauled out on the Scottish coast. The muzzle is shorter than that of the grey seal with a dip between the forehead and nose tip.

trio from the boat on previous days in other parts of the marsh with little reaction as long as we did not stop and approach. The sight of occasional boats going past in the narrow waterways is acceptable to the seals and very like the familiarity with cars gained by deer in parks and game animals in the East African National Parks.

If the common seal is typical of muddy estuaries and sandbanks, the grey seal is more associated with rugged, rocky shores. Both can be found in each of the types of habitat and careful observation is needed.

The diagrams show the principal differences in the shape of the head and nostrils. If you do not live near the sea, I do urge you to watch seals on your holidays by the coast. Boats can be taken to particular sites such as the Farne Islands. The behaviour of seals in the water and their interaction on land is of interest. Bull grey seal territories and the relationships of cows to pups are intriguing and a highly complex subject in their own right. Breeding colonies are established ashore in the autumn and

Figure 115 The different head features of the grey seal (left) and common seal in diagrammatic form. The bull grey seal is very thick in the neck and has a pronounced roman nose.

Figure 116 A grey seal pup suckles its cow on a rocky breeding beach in Scotland.

are more easily watched in the grey than in the common seal. Bulls fight for dominance over a rocky beach and defend their cows from rivals. The bull thus defends the beach which may contain several recently born pups, but his interest is in the cows who come ashore to feed their young at intervals. They are mated by the bull as they come into oestrous at this time. Common seals pup earlier, in midsummer, and are generally more difficult to watch out on the sandbanks. Some of their nurseries

Figure 117 A large bull grey seal; note its bulk, the long, straight nose and widely separated nostrils.

are in the rocky types of coast where the grey seals pup and can thus be observed from above. Lactation is brief, little more than a month in duration, but the pups grow rapidly and the attractive white juvenile then fends for itself in the sea, making the transition from a rich milk diet to small live food such as fish, prawns or shrimps. The grey seal pup is solitary, but common seal young play and swim together off the nursery grounds. Combined with the beauty of the surroundings and walking in such areas, you will be repaid for your efforts, whatever the weather.

# 9 Keeping the record straight

Watching mammals has practical applications to science and natural history. Observations are not of value if unshared and left to fade in old notebooks. There is a network of often old established Natural History Societies easily traced through county libraries. (My own area is covered by the Hertfordshire Natural History Society which has published the records and observations made in the county since 1875.)

I recommend membership of your local society and you may be willing to become the recorder of mammals if the job is not already being done. There is a tendency for some Natural History Societies to be over-scientific or perhaps pseudo-scientific and consider only those projects which involve particular equipment and excessive data as worthwhile in outdoor work. Yet the membership is generally made up of enthusiastic amateurs who love being out in the countryside. It is *accuracy* of observation and careful recording which adds to our knowledge of wildlife. You need not feel any obligation to do more than record distribution data and this is what I want to deal with in the following pages.

A glance outside your window and the observation that a mole is making hills in your lawn can contribute a new area for the distribution of this common mammal should you trouble to forward it to the right quarters. Local societies collate distribution material and forward this to the Biological Records Centre at Monks Wood, Huntingdon (see Appendix III). At the time of writing, Henry Arnold is recording all such material.

The Mammal Society (see Appendix III) is an excellent national body concerned with the publication of accurate scientific literature on mammals and the dissemination of this information through its meetings and symposia. It produces a variety of publications and advises government bodies as well as the media on mammal matters. It maintains its neutral, advisory position very carefully and as a result has the reputation of unbiased information on which decisions for management on mammals can be based.

There is such a great need for research into all our wildlife and the inter-relationships between animals and plants in natural communities that the encouragement of such work is an important aim of the Society.

---

Figure 118 Although streams, lakes, rivers and the coast provide the focus for most otter activity, they may feed and travel extensively over land.

Many members are professional workers in this field who use a variety of technical aids, but this does not mean that accurate, observed information from amateurs is any less valuable. The essential attribute is self-criticism and the ability not to jump to conclusions. Bad amateur observation is useless, but good, careful descriptive work will always be of value.

The Deer Society has already been mentioned. The various conservation bodies are very worthy of our support (see Appendix III). Your local County Naturalists' Trust will welcome anyone with mammal interests in its membership, and addresses can be obtained from the Society for the Promotion of Nature Conservation, and the national and international bodies such as the Fauna and Flora Preservation Society and World Wildlife Fund are doing very important work for mammal conservation and management. A good society is a source of information to curious and enthusiastic naturalists who want to know all they can about the wildlife they love to watch. Half the value of activities such as the Mammal Society weekends held at a different regional centre each year is the contact with fellow enthusiasts. The papers read and the countryside visited are of course important, but the discussions away from the lecture hall can teach so much.

The first thing you will need to record your mammal observations is a set of local maps. If you do not already read maps easily this should come with practice. Explore with constant reference to the Ordnance Surveys of the area. Two sizes are useful: the typical OS 1 : 50,000 with a pink cover and the OS 25,000 with a blue one. The first are general purpose rambling and touring maps, but if you are spending any length of time in an area, the latter scale is essential. It is of a size where badger sets and good sites for deer, for example, can be pinpointed in detail. When visiting areas such as Wales and Scotland, the touring maps such as Bartholomew's 'Grand Touring' series are very useful to see the broad area of a country. In Ireland the Dublin Ordnance Survey gives a map for the whole island and there are the 1 : 250,000 regional maps for Great Britain. European equivalents can also be purchased in this country (see Appendix III).

The maps will enable you to locate your records with a grid reference and it is most important that this becomes second nature to you, (see figure 120). The first thing to do when you find a rabbit skull, for example, is to note the grid reference and date. If you collect found material such as skulls, start off with a simple numbering system for everything which comes in. You will need a notebook and may like to add your initials to the record; the first object in my notebook is M.C./1. With the relevant data listed alongside and this number on the skull, you will always be able to trace its origin, date and any other notes.

---

Figure 119 Common dolphins swimming in formation on the bow waves alongside a ship at sunset.

1

2

(1) A road casualty weasel is noted with location and date.

(2) Site is fixed on Ordnance Survey map, sheet code TL.

To find grid reference correct to 100m, take west edge of the 1km square in which record occurred, 21, and count off in tenths eastwards:

$$\frac{\begin{array}{r} TL21 \\ 4 \end{array}}{TL214}$$

Take south edge of the square, in this case 19, and count off in tenths northwards:3. This gives 193 and the full 6 figure grid reference TL214/193.

(3 and 4) Records can be published on a county basis or |(5)| nationally. County maps can be 1km or (as 3) 2km squares. Local records should be sent to the Biological Records Centre (see Appendix III) for the 10km national scheme.

(5) A section of the 1960-70 weasel map. Circles indicate pre-1960 records.

Figure 120 Recording grid references.

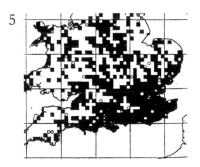

3

Weasel *Mustela nivalis*

4

Guide to the 10 km squares

5

The distribution of mammals is something we can all help record. In our county we work on a 2x2 km square system and this scale gives a useful, quick visual guide to the occurrence of particular mammals on a county basis through publication of the maps from time to time. Why a county basis? Well, this is as good as any other arbitrary boundary you might like to draw to limit your area of study. I am in favour of county schemes because they encourage the interest many people have in their particular area. If you say this is the first record for Hertfordshire, for example, anyone can immediately picture a given area.

My own approach is to keep a daily diary so that any observation is recorded the same day it was made. I stick in pictures and add grid references and can always trace back to a particular event. I have found my diaries (which go back every day to 1960; with over 7,300 entries so far) have helped greatly in the preparation of this book. Little incidents should not be allowed to slip past unconsidered as they may well fall into a pattern. Your diaries will always be there, as long as you store them safely, to follow observations through.

Figure 121 Field notebooks with sketches (top left) and daily diaries with photographs and drawings freely added to the text.

You do not have to write every day up, (although I do as a general diary), just as long as the information is there on the right day. I favour the A5 size of diary, well bound and freely available each autumn in the large stationery chain stores. It is also useful to keep a set of maps on cards with a grid imposed on them, one for each species, so that you can fill in a new square as the records come in. These are available from some local Natural History Societies. A large tetrad guide is very useful in transferring the information and I prefer a numerical squared-up sheet for this. You may be content to keep records for yourself and send a summary to the recorders for your local Natural History Society. If you become a recorder yourself, you will find that this is a specialist activity with a responsibility to all the other recorders in the area and that you have to organise and publish the records. The transference of a record to a grid reference with a date and other data and the stages involved are illustrated in figure 120.

The maps can be made up into the appropriate size for the page text areas of your local society's journal and published in blocks of, say, six or eight to a page. This encourages interest and brings in more records from other naturalists who may be principally interested in birds or flowers, but see that their records of mammals will help complete the picture of distribution.

Records are best kept in box files as a card system and a printed type has great advantages. My local society has made up particular sheets for different branches of work such as the bat survey and small mammal surveys. The great thing is to try to keep things in order and not waste all those observations. Publish original information as often as you can. If you are not used to writing up material, seek advice from other members of your society. There are certain basic rules to follow.

Manuscripts should be double line spaced with wide margins on each side for corrections. Be concise and keep to factual, clear statements; do not make deductions unless the evidence is there. Send the manuscript carbon around to colleagues for their criticisms and comments. Always make a carbon or photocopy to keep at home. If you have checked published references, make out a bibliography (see how these should be set out at the end of this book) and acknowledge any help you have been given during the work or its preparation as a paper.

It helps in this routine of recording work to have a box of gadgets so that you are not forever looking for the tape measure or pen. I use an old slide box and whenever a dead animal turns up, I make the standard measurements using the following items: the record sheets, scale, steel tape measure, set of Pesola scales (available from the British Trust for Ornithology, see Appendix III, who supply bird ringers: expensive, but indispensable for accurate small measurements of weights), forceps, pens, thermometer, micrometer and tubes for ectoparasites. The standard measurements are illustrated in figure 122. It is also useful to have tapered plastic bags (with a small air gap at the thin end) to keep a live small mammal relatively quiet during weighing. On the Pesola scales I use the following weights: a 50 g one for bats; a 300 g for mammals up to about rat size; 1000 g, 10 kg and 25 kg for rabbits through to badgers. For heavier mammals such as deer, I use large scales typical of a game dealer's cold store.

If you collect a great deal of data on one particular species and wish to

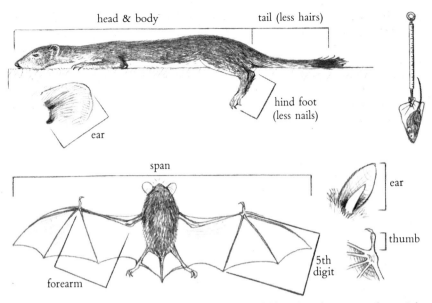

Figure 122 The standard measurements which should be taken for mammals; weight and sex should also be recorded. In bats the thumb and ear length can be added.

examine the results these figures may give, I recommend that you approach professional workers and investigate the use of a computer. It is relatively easy to skin fresh mammal specimens and the Mammal Society has published good guides to this work in the first edition of the *Handbook* (1964) and in a more recent *Mammal Review* (1977). Always use fresh scalpel blades and follow strict standards of hygiene to avoid infection from the dead material.

Flat skins on cards or tanned, cured skins can be stored for future reference. I have collected seventeen badger skins from road casualties over the years and have a number of card skins as well as fox, deer and mounted species. This is a very interesting branch of mammal study and encourages an interest in taxidermy.

# 10 Moments of time

Written records are an essential part of your mammal watching if you wish your observations to be of value to others or to yourself at a later date. Recording by camera, tape and drawing is an extension of this activity.

In many ways I am loath to recommend photography or the use of a tape-recorder to anyone who enjoys going out and simply watching. There is so much commercial pressure to buy expensive equipment and there are so many pitfalls when you have your cameras and recorders. A mass of unsorted slides and unedited tapes are of little use, yet may represent hours of work and much expense in equipment and materials. You should not undertake these activities lightly, but of the three, drawing is the cheapest and will commit you to the least expensive equipment. I have written about all these subjects in this chapter to help newcomers as well as to offer a viewpoint to experienced practitioners. Try never to let your equipment conflict with watching. As you build up your collection of slides and tapes, file them away in alphabetical subject order in the case of slides or with written-up descriptions of the sounds recorded. The easiest way to locate the position on the tape of each original recording is by use of the recorder's numbering counter.

Everyone should draw or at least be able to sketch out observations and prepare simple line diagrams or graphs. Just as you should use the best films and tapes you can get, use the best quality drawing equipment and the correct materials. Line drawing in ink on cheap mounting board or using wash on thin cartridge paper can only cause poor results and frustration.

I have limited experience of film making, but enough to know that it is a specialist activity which stands on its own. Still photography and tape can be combined with general watching, but worthwhile films are complex productions which must have a structure or story. Eric Ashby has shown what can be achieved by patient dedication to this study. Moving pictures are very useful for mammal study, but slow motion studies of deer or bats in flight are the sort of projects best left to professionals; the expertise it demands may mean you have to give up general watching to concentrate on it. It looks as if home video films will be developed to a very useful stage in the next few years. When filming is reduced to simple miniature cassettes and cameras I expect they will be commonplace and another valuable aid to recording our wildlife observations.

## Still photography

Still photography has endless applications and there is always the hope of seeing your work in print or the prospect of giving talks illustrated with your own transparencies to spur you on, in addition to having a personal record of your observations.

Top quality natural history photography is one of the most demanding and complex of all forms of photography. What sort of camera should you choose? You will find that the professionals all have individual requirements and also that fashions and favours in camera makes, particularly in the single lens reflex (SLR) 35 mm field, vary from country to country. In North America the top selling four or five cameras are different from Britain's, which in turn differ from those used in Europe. Most wild mammal photographers use Hasselblads or Bronicas and combine these $2\frac{1}{4}$ in (6 × 6 cm) format cameras with 35 mm systems like Olympus, Pentax and Nikon. The Pentax 6 × 7 cm format also has great attractions as you are more likely to use the whole transparency area if it is a rectangle in its original form. The important thing for the amateur is to keep to a system once it has been decided upon and to save for each carefully chosen stage. I learnt the basics of photography with a little non-SLR 35 mm Agfa Silette and you may find that a simple and reasonably priced pocket type camera is adequate for your watching days.

While I implore you not to fall for the technology band wagon, it is nevertheless true that you can now buy top quality and very advanced electronic equipment at prices which are still reasonable. My first Canon gave me the chance to interchange different types of lens and see exactly what I was taking by viewing through the lens. Through-the-lens metering in modern cameras now gives a great degree of accuracy, especially for colour transparencies where exposure is so critical. Although I have used Rolliflex and Linhoff cameras (4 × 5 in), I nearly always rely now on a Canon for my 35 mm system. I now have two fully automatic Canon A1s with five exposure modes and the AE1 (see figure 123). The advantages are many but include automatic flash control and the ability to powerwind the film.

Initially I missed the ability to adjust the exposure by setting the needle in the viewfinder. It is easy in direct sunlight or with a bright subject to underexpose by a stop to kill the glare. With the automatic camera you have to do this non-visually, on the top setting and it took time to get used to this. The main advantage, however, for wild mammal photography is the way the camera will adjust to constantly changing lighting conditions. You may have spent hours waiting for a stoat to run out from the edge of woodland. Perhaps several days have been spent previously on research into where it can be found. You may have only

Figure 123 A 35mm camera system (Canon and Vivitar) assembled by the author for mammal and general wildlife photography. On the tripods, left to right: AE1 camera (for black-and-white film), powerwinder on 600mm telephoto lens; A1 (for slow colour), automatic bellows and 90mm macro lens; flashgun and diffuser. In the aluminium boxes from left to right: 35–70mm zoom lens; 28mm lens; A1 (for fast colour), power winder, 75–150mm zoom; matched multipliers; lens brush; 50mm lens; silver umbrella flash (part); films; two converters; spare batteries; flash extension cables; spike for ground level photography; flashgun; 18 different filters; 300mm lens; 10m remote cable release; matched 292 flashguns.

twenty seconds when a stoat appears and goes on its way and it may run through four or five lighting conditions in that time. You will have enough worries focusing and getting the animal composed in the frame, but if you are also having to adjust the exposure, valuable time is lost. With the fully automatic camera and a powerwinder or motor drive you could have a choice of ten or more transparencies as opposed to two or three incorrectly exposed ones. All natural history photographers go through the frustrations of camera and equipment faults which give undeserved poor results after a great deal of effort and it is worth choosing reliable cameras and flashguns.

On the choice of a lens system, I use two zooms: a 35–70 mm macro Vivitar (for general work) and for badger photography a small 70–150 mm Vivitar. This has separate focus and zoom rings enabling you to focus on a set entrance or play area in the evening light and then zoom in and out in the dark, long after it is possible to focus again, adjusting to whether an individual badger or a group have come out. I have the standard Canon lens, (never snub the 50 mm standard focal length which is often useful for wildlife work), a 28 mm and hope to add a 20 mm and 15 mm full-frame fish-eye wide-angle in time. Wide-angle lenses have great potential in habitat and plant studies. My most exceptional lens for definition is the Series I 90 mm Macro Vivitar. I also have the 300 mm Vivitar and Series I 600 mm Vivitar mirror lens. When choosing a new lens or lens system I recommend you to try out as many versions as possible. If you can borrow and test on film, so much the better.

A powerwinder or motor drive unit extends the use of the camera considerably and is to be recommended if you wish to specialise in natural history work. I have already mentioned how useful repeated shots of an animal in the brief time you may have can improve your chances of having at least one or two successful pictures. For wildlife work there are advantages you might not realise until you have a power-winder on the camera. When taking flash photographs of mice in captivity I found that the duration of the modern electronic flash did not disturb them, but my hand rewinding did. By switching on the power-winder each picture was taken without any movement or disturbance from the camera area and I obtained a sequence of a mouse washing without the animal running for cover at each exposure.

I have even used the powerwinder to catch the attention of a fox stalking chickens. I noticed the fox sunning itself by a thicket edge about 100 metres from our garden and ran indoors to get the camera and a 600 mm lens. When I re-emerged with the camera on a tripod, I saw that the fox had got up and was stalking next door's free-range hens. It would have gone round behind some huts out of sight had I not taken a quick picture. The sound of the powerwinder made it stop and after a few moments it ambled back towards the thicket edge. I took a series of pictures and managed to get a group of geese in the foreground with fox behind in two frames. It was midday, the sun was behind me and as the fox had settled down with half closed eyes, I decided to try my luck at approaching. I had a light shirt on and I took two pictures as I approached through the geese. I do not think the fox could distinguish the white shapes very clearly until my last steady picture from the tripod at about fifty paces. It ran off and my last photograph is of a ginger blurr.

The question of choosing the type of film to use is a complex one. You will need to use a brand of film a great deal before you know all its good and bad points. Try out as many as you can and make up your own mind. I use Kodachrome 25, Ektachrome 200 and the new 100 ASA Agfa Professional as my colour films for different situations and Ilford FP4 (125 ASA) black-and-white film. If it were possible I would use Kodachrome 25 all the time for colour work but it is too slow for many wildlife subjects. (Slow, fine grain films produce the sharpest results but can only be used in very bright lighting conditions.)

High contrasts in sunlight can be subdued with filters and half-chrome coloured filters and colour accents combined with polarising filters can be very useful. I use colour most of the time because black-and-white copies can be made if necessary. I have found that copies made in the darkroom are liable to be too contrasty and it is easier to run through your selected slides on a slide duplicator with black-and-white film in the copying camera. The results are adequate for general book and magazine reproduction, but you cannot beat a sharp black-and-white original.

Flash photography is an essential part of mammal photography as there are so many situations when artificial light is needed. The traditional positioning of flashguns around your subjects can readily be found in the camera books. Side lighting can be very effective and back lighting too, with remote sensors to fire the gun from another flash on or near the camera. I use five flashguns: a Canon 199A, Vivitar 283, 365 and 292 types. You should test your flashguns and find out the best lighting effects and the quality of each particular type. Bounce flash gives a very soft, flat light and a diffuser card attachment to the flashgun helps to improve the result. There is a problem with macro work where the flash is too powerful for the object in close-up. This is why I favour the long working distance of the 90 mm macro. Canon do an automatic macro flash matched to their very sharp 80–200 zoom with two flash heads around the end of the lens.

Figure 124 Two flashguns (Vivitar 292s) set upright and on the side to give maximum cover. One is connected to a camera, one triggered by a remote sensor as the exposure is made.

Figure 125 Stalking roe deer with a camera: A doe is called up with a squeak lure when fawns are present in cover and rushes towards the source of the sound. A tree is useful to steady the lens. In this type of photography quite small telephotos can be adequate; slower, larger lenses give a bigger image but camera shake is more likely.

Only use flash on the camera if it is positioned high enough not to reflect the light from the eyes of animals back into your lens. This gives unpleasant golden or red eyes in nocturnal subjects. I have found that the 199A (which works from the 'hot shoe' on top of the camera) does not cause this flare back unless taken at low level in line with the eyes and is very useful for general photography. When I took a whole series of pictures of a polecat litter it meant awkward viewpoints into a straw box. The automatic control through the lens gave the right exposure each time. When used with the other flashguns the camera exposes correctly, but you can angle the flash head upwards if you do not want direct light from the camera position.

Automatic flash exposure is a definite advantage. It is still easy to take very badly lit pictures with automatic equipment, but whether bounced or direct or used in conjunction with other flash heads, the automatic camera gives well exposed results. Use rechargeable batteries for your flash and powerwinder equipment and have a spare set always charged up in your camera bag.

I store everything in aluminium boxes, which are strong enough to sit on. It may seem best for wildlife work to have the black aluminium type, but these do absorb heat and in sunlight you may cook your films inside. Throw an old coat or cloth over the box if there is a risk of animals seeing the bright metal. A simple, inconspicuous bag over the shoulder is adequate for many occasions.

Tripods are essential to prevent camera shake and you may end up with three or four if undertaking complicated light and light-beam automatic trigger types of photography. The newer types can flatten very well and adapt to almost ground level which can help you to achieve more attractive compositions. I have a 10 metre-long cable release which allows use of the camera without attention by remote control. The infra-red remote control of the shutter release does not seem necessary unless you need a very high speed response.

Try to develop an eye for a picture and look at pictures as often as possible. Magazines such as the *National Geographic Magazine* and the photography yearbooks help with composition and viewpoints. Even using the best equipment, perfectly exposed pictures of delightful subjects can be dull because of poor composition or camera angle.

You may consider having your work published. The 35 mm SLR camera system is now very much a part of modern publishing but its progress has more to do with improved emulsions than with lens quality. The 35 mm photograph must be pin-sharp, perfectly exposed and should fill the whole transparency area to be considered. If all these requirements are fulfilled it is no longer second best to the $2\frac{1}{4}$ in ($6 \times 6$ cm) transparency. Colour prints are not generally used in printing. If you want to get colour work published, you should always use transparencies.

You can crop transparencies with a mask very effectively by lengths of black light-proof line tape made by Chartpak or Letraset which covers in different widths. It is normally used by designers who have to produce lines of standard width above the normal drawing pen sizes or where curves are easier to produce by tape. It has a clean edge and sticks well. Never use insulation tape.

If you are starting out, do not just read wildlife photography books although I strongly recommend Leonard Warner's *Mammal Photography and Observation* and Heather Angel's *Nature Photography*. Harold Evans' *Pictures on a Page* is largely about photo-journalism and it links with graphics. It is excellent on aspects of composition and choosing the right moment to take a picture. It is full of memorable observations such as that the 35 mm camera is a different camera when it is used on a tripod, or that lack of sharpness is usually the result of a slight movement as the picture is taken rather than the lens quality or film emulsion.

# Giving talks

Giving illustrated talks is very rewarding and you will learn a great deal in the course of them. I have been given many useful mammal records by people who have stopped for a chat afterwards. I also feel that one is helping wild mammals by showing them in their natural habitats, with reference to their value in the ecology of a particular area.

Your choice of projector depends on the demands you are going to put on it. I began to do talks on mammals regularly and after a couple of near misses, the machine completely jammed during a talk, damaging a slide. A replacement had to be found whilst the audience waited and I resolved to purchase my own Kodak Carousel projector and take it everywhere. In eight years of regular use, I have never had projection failure with the Carousel. The gravity feed is virtually foolproof and a spare bulb is always clipped inside the projector. I keep the projector on the car seat rather than in the boot where the bulb might jarr and break. At home it is always set up pointing onto a sheet of white card in my little work room so that I can go through slides at a moment's notice, day or night.

Through long experience I now take plug socket adaptors, extension cables and put a zoom lens on the projector, but I always ask for a screen to be provided.

The Carousel slide carriers are useful as a form of slide storage in themselves and I eventually came to divide subjects for talks up into: 'Mammals of Hertfordshire', 'Bats', 'Muntjac', 'Badgers' and so forth. Preparation time is, however, considerable unless you use an identical (and therefore boring) talk each time. I prefer never to use notes. You can add to your 'moment of time' by recordings. The roar of a red stag and the scream of a fox will lend atmosphere to your colour slides.

You can venture into combined slide/tape productions using two or more Carousels linked with tape so that the pictures fade in and out. Multi-screen shows can be very effective, but you multiply your problems in terms of equipment and I would advise taking some kind of audio-visual course first.

Slide storage in alphabetical order and a light box for sorting and examining slides under a × 5 or × 10 lens will become essential with greater use of your collection. I prefer English classification although a lot of flowers and fungi, for example, may call for Latin subdivisions. All go into standard twenty-four slide plastic files in a filing cabinet. They are in total darkness, dust free and I can trace an individual slide amongst the 8,000 or so in a very short time. You can subdivide each heading into, for example: 'Badgers: habitats', 'Badgers: family groups' and so on.

## Sound recording

We have briefly considered using sound recording and it is in some ways a more vivid way of recalling moments spent out in the wild than using pictures. Cassette recorders have simplified problems of tape-recording quite considerably, but for top quality results the portable reel-to-reel types are widely used. You will see Nagra tape-recorders used by the television and radio companies but many top amateur recorders go to this expense, too. The Uher Report recorders are much cheaper, very strong and reliable portables and are widely used in broadcasting and natural history work.

The automatic types can have pitfalls and it is wise not to use the automatic setting for mammal sounds. You will often be recording sudden bursts of sound which can cause a surge of sound adjustment. For example, when a fox barks the recorder will rapidly adjust to the loud noise. Then, in the silence which follows, the automatic control seeks out the slightest sound in the distance. At the next bark, the sequence is repeated, giving an unpleasant effect. It is better to set your recorder manually to the right level.

I have only used a parabola to concentrate the sound into the microphone, but there are a number of new pistol-grip 'gun' microphones which exclude extraneous sounds very efficiently and are easy to handle. Wind noise and movement cause more problems than anything else and it is best to use a parabola on a tripod with a mask of acoustically transparent foam (see figure 125). To avoid bumps and crashes do not move the cable after recording has commenced. It is best clipped to the side of your parabola or looped and held with the microphone in hand-held work. You quickly become aware of the extraneous noises which harass the sound recordist. Aircraft noise and motorcycles are just two such delights.

My most amusing incident when recording mammals was when a badger tried to bury the microphone in disgust. A young boar had mated with a more mature sow in the set repeatedly through one February, to his obvious noisy pleasure and I had finally got the microphone against a tree close to the favoured entrance where they usually occupied themselves. During my recording, the boar left the sow and came grumbling up to the microphone, scratching angrily at the soil around it. It then turned, dug a heap of leaves and leaf mould back over the microphone

Figure 126 A parabola fitted with a microphone on a tripod. The acoustically transparent foam windshield has been removed and is at the rear. The microphone is linked to either reel-to-reel mono or cassette stereo portable tape-recorders.

with a few disagreeable kicks and then stamped off back into the set with more whickering grumbles. You may wish to sell some of the sounds you record: if so do remember to aim for quality and record at the fastest possible speed as this produces the best quality result.

It is best to write out a list of subjects as you finish each tape, giving dates and locations against the numbering system. I edit my reels onto cassettes for talks and have found the ferri-chrome type very faithful to the originals. They are perfectly adequate to fill a hall with mammal sounds. Figure 127 illustrates two applications of the tape-recorder: using the parabola in the field and introducing the microphone into a bat roost.

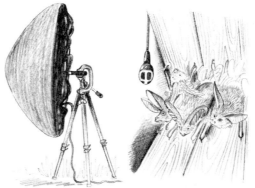

Figure 127 Left: Acoustically transparent foam held over the parabola by elastic for use as a windshield in the field. Right: A microphone lowered into a bat roost next to the colony to record sound.

If you have recorded something you think is outstanding, you cannot do better than contact the BBC Natural History Unit in Bristol (BBC Broadcasting House, Whiteladies Road, Bristol BS8 2LR). The producers of the wildlife radio programmes may be prepared to listen to your tape and you should initially send a letter with a self-addressed and stamped envelope to ask if they are interested in a certain subject. Never worry about editing the tape. If the producers wish to hear the recording, send the original and they can organise any archive copy work necessary.

The annual competition for wildlife sound is a very worthwhile activity to enter if you have some good results to offer. The standards are very high and categories include stereo. I have never gone to the extra trouble of stereo work for wildlife sounds, but some interesting effects can be obtained. The competition is organised by 3M UK Limited, 3M House, Wigmore Street, London W1A 1ET.

# Drawing

The value of a sketch has been referred to in Chapter 9. A sketch can say so much in a few lines and capture the essence of an observation far more immediately than the written word. One of the most attractive books written on badgers is the little-known, but beautifully illustrated *When Badgers Wake* by Eileen Soper, unfortunately never reprinted after its first appearance in the 1950s. The illustrations are sensitive, well observed pencil drawings which capture the atmosphere of badger watching perfectly. Although the authoress never reveals the locality of the set, I was doing set survey work twelve years later and the drawings were so good that I recognised the cliff of chalk and dead elm from her drawings. Soil has fallen away from below one of the oaks, but the surroundings are very much the same now, twenty-five years on.

You do not have to be a Soper, or indeed a Thorburn or a Lodge to record basic illustrative points. You will however find that some of the best illustrations of mammals are in Millais' *Mammals of Great Britain and Ireland* and it is Millais' sketches of hedgehogs swimming and the accuracy of Lodge's bat paintings for example which contribute so much to our study of these animals. Refer to this type of work, but do not be discouraged by its high standard.

It is best to use the pen with which you write your notes for your drawings. Modern fountain pens will take black cartridge ink which is durable and stable. The use of the pen in everyday sketches gives confidence. Use pencils of about B or 2B softness, but if you are preparing a well finished pencil drawing, a whole range from 6H to 6B may come in useful. The Caran d'Ache colour pencils which can be softened with water on the page give a mixture of pencil qualities and watercolour combined.

Most observers of wildlife want to reproduce their observations in line when drawing and it is the range of pens which is most confusing. In the same way that faster or slower films with their respective advantages and disadvantages are available in photography, you also have various strengths of inks from the weak 'permanent' black fountain pen inks which do not reproduce well and turn blue when mixed with water, to the very strong 'indian' inks which dry waterproof and hard and give a very black image for process work. In between these is the Rotring type of ink which can be used in pens without clogging as long as the pen is cleaned regularly. This type of ink for the barrel nib type of drawing pens gives the strength of blackness without the weakness of the fountain black. When you have to use process white paint to take out a section of an ink drawing, the thin fountain pen inks can stain and show up through the white.

Much of the correction to inked line drawing is done by a scalpel blade. The Rotring ink can also be scratched as well as indian ink, leaving a sharp edge. As long as you use a good line board such as CS10 or Academy line board by Oram and Robinson, you can scratch away the surface of the board without furring the card surface. You can redraw over and correct again on the best boards and the scratching in itself can give tone and shading to an illustration. So do not expect to produce good results on a

Figure 128 A range of materials used by the author for line illustration. A reducing glass (looks like a magnifying glass here) is useful to show how work will reduce.

piece of cheap board which powders if scratched by a blade and cannot be reworked.

A dip pen and indian ink are very useful for free, illustrative types of drawing where variety in the width of your pen line gives interest to the drawing. The Rotring types of pen are excellent for exact, equal line width work and give a constant width essential in more technical illustrations and graphics. They do not, however, lend themselves to free line drawing because of the monotony of the line. You will find the drawing pen sets available now give a fountain pen ease of use with black ink for reproduction.

A new pen has recently become available which gives very fine detail and yet retains the variety of line: the brushpen. It is a fine, pointed brush made by Edding with a constant supply of ink as in a fibre tip. I am uncertain if the ink is permanent, but it looks very satisfactory and I have already used it in book work. You can go from the finest line to a thick brush-like effect in moments.

Remember that if you can draw a rough square and circle you have the basis for drawing anything. Do progress to watercolours and the easier oil colours. Mammals make excellent subjects and you can project your favourite colour slide onto a canvas and paint round it. Do not rely on photographs too much for copying purposes however. Photographs have their place for reference and in many cases to reproduce the proportions of wild animals you require exact information, but if you take up drawing and painting seriously, attend classes and learn to observe

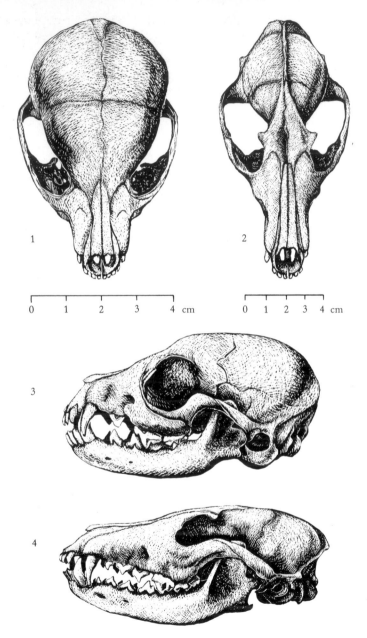

Figure 129 Scraperboard can suit some subjects such as bones. The considerable change in the shape of a fox skull from a six-week-old cub (1) dorsal view and (3) ventral view to a mature adult (2) and (4) is emphasised by showing both skulls the same size. (Material: Dr Stephen Harris).

from what is in front of you. Purely photographic-based or mechanically traced drawing has a flatness and lack of character which even the finest rendering techniques cannot hide.

You might also try using designer's gouache and the various techniques of the air-brush. The latter needs much practice and cannot be learnt in an hour or two. Both gouache and air-brush work should be sprayed over to fix the paint and prevent damage to the surface in transit or by rubbing against papers in the studio. A spray such as the Letraset type to fix instant lettering (Letracote) is ideal. The air-brush requires film masks to stop paint or ink being sprayed onto background areas. Layers of colour can be built-up as new areas are cut by scalpel and then painted. Preparation time can be prolonged, but this technique can give a special unity to a picture or series of pictures. Very even grades of tone can be achieved very quickly once the masking has been made ready. Care must be taken in spraying to give fine grades of texture and the equipment must be kept very clean to prevent clogging and splatter. It always looks darker when you take away the masking so do not over-work by accident.

As can be seen from many of the diagram illustrations in this book, you can be as simple as you like as long as your lines are clear and show a point visually. Drawing as you watch mammals can be difficult, but it is very satisfying. Even sketching our own deer at home can be frustrating as the animals constantly move, but sketches on the spot can say a great deal when you refer to them later.

## Final thoughts

I have no hesitation in encouraging people to watch mammals as long as this activity is carried out responsibly. Films, television and books have transformed human interest in wildlife in the last thirty years and more and more people find recreation in observation of the natural world.

Mammals, as we have seen, are difficult to study but they are some of the most rewarding of natural subjects. They are also some of the most endangered. The conservation of whales involves international politics and major economic decisions. Disease such as bovine tuberculosis in badgers in parts of southwest England and rabies in foxes in Europe involve governments in vital management strategies. Otters may become absent from great areas of Europe in future years due to the chemical pollution of waters, which leaves toxic residues in their food. The hunting of our larger mammals is always subject for debate. Mammals are in the news constantly and the silent watcher has a part to play in all this. It is knowledge and observation which provides the basis for all proper management. Watch with patience, but above all, with love for your subject.

# Appendix I Classification

The English names referred to in the text are listed here with their Latin classification. If you are not familiar with the way plants and animals are classified the following notes may give a brief introduction.

Every mammal is given a genus and species name in Latin. Two or more mammals may be very similar and be grouped in the same genus, for example the common and pygmy shrews are *Sorex araneus* and *Sorex minutus*. The genus is always given with an initial capital letter but the species is always in lower case type. The name of the first person to describe the animal may be added, as in (L) for Linnaeus. In manuscripts Latin names of species should be underlined to indicate they are to be set in italic type.

Interesting notes on this subject can be found in the *Handbook* (1977). A. F. Gotch also goes into the background to mammal classification in *Mammals – Their Latin Names Explained* (1979). The main groupings for a mammal begin with Kingdom (Animal) Subkingdom, Phylum, Subphylum, Superclass, Class, Subclass, Superorder, Order, Suborder, Superfamily, Family, Subfamily, Genus, Subgenus, Species and may end with Subspecies or Race. Subspecies is not always used, nor are all the divisions, but they are available as circumstances dictate. The major groupings below are the eleven orders covered in this book:

| | |
|---|---|
| **Order** Marsupialia | marsupials |
| **Family** Macropodidae | kangaroos and wallabies |
| *Macropus rufogriseus* | red-necked wallaby |
| | |
| **Order** Insectivora | insectivores |
| **Family** Erinaceidae | |
| *Erinaceus europaeus* | hedgehog |
| **Family** Talpidae | |
| *Talpa europaea* | mole |
| **Family** Soricidae | shrews |
| *Sorex araneus* | common shrew |
| *Sorex minutus* | pygmy shrew |
| *Neomys fodiens* | water shrew |
| *Crocidura russula* | greater white-toothed shrew |
| *Crocidura suaveolens* | lesser white-toothed shrew |
| | |
| **Order** Chiroptera | bats |
| **Family** Rhinolophidae | horseshoe bats |
| *Rhinolophus ferrumequinum* | greater horseshoe bat |
| *Rhinolophus hipposideros* | lesser horseshoe bat |
| **Family** Vespertilionidae | |
| *Myotis mystacinus* | whiskered bat |
| *Myotis brandti* | Brandt's bat |
| *Myotis nattereri* | Natterer's bat |
| *Myotis bechsteini* | Bechstein's bat |
| *Myotis myotis* | mouse-eared bat |
| *Myotis daubentoni* | Daubenton's bat |
| *Eptesicus serotinus* | serotine |

| | |
|---|---|
| *Nyctalus leisleri* | Leisler's bat |
| *Nyctalus noctula* | noctule |
| *Pipistrellus pipistrellus* | pipistrelle |
| *Pipistrellus nathusii* | Nathusius' pipistrelle |
| *Barbastella barbastellus* | barbastelle |
| *Plecotus auritus* | common long-eared bat |
| *Plecotus austriacus* | grey long-eared bat |
| | |
| **Order** Lagomorpha | lagomorphs |
| **Family** Leporidae | rabbits and hares |
| *Oryctolagus cuniculus* | rabbit |
| *Lepus capensis* | brown hare |
| *Lepus timidus* | mountain hare |
| | |
| **Order** Rodentia | rodents |
| **Family** Sciuridae | squirrels |
| *Sciurus vulgaris* | red squirrel |
| *Sciurus carolinensis* | grey squirrel |
| **Family Cricetidae** | voles |
| **Subfamily** Microtinae | |
| *Clethrionomys glareolus* | bank vole |
| *Microtus agrestis* | field vole |
| *Microtus arvalis* | Orkney/Guernsey voles |
| *Arvicola terrestris* | water vole |
| **Family** Muridae | rats and mice |
| *Apodemus sylvaticus* | wood mouse |
| *Apodemus flavicollis* | yellow-necked mouse |
| *Micromys minutus* | harvest mouse |
| *Mus musculus* | house mouse |
| *Rattus rattus* | ship rat |
| *Rattus norvegicus* | brown rat |
| **Family** Gliridae | dormice |
| *Glis glis* | fat dormouse |
| *Muscardinus avellanarius* | common dormouse |
| **Family** Capromyidae | |
| *Myocastor coypus* | coypu |
| | |
| **Order** Cetacea | whales |
| **Suborder** Mysticeti | baleen whales |
| **Family** Balaenidae | right whales |
| *Balaena glacialis* | black right whale |
| **Family** Balaenopteridae | rorquals |
| *Megaptera novaeangliae* | humpback whale |
| *Balaenoptera physalus* | common rorqual |
| *Balaenoptera acutorostrata* | minke |
| *Balaenoptera borealis* | sei whale |
| *Balaenoptera musculus* | blue whale |
| **Suborder** Odontoceti | toothed whales |
| **Family** Physeteridae | sperm whales |
| *Physeter catodon* | sperm whale |

| | |
|---|---|
| *Kogia breviceps* | pygmy sperm whale |
| **Family** Ziphiidae | beaked whales |
| *Hyperoodon ampullatus* | bottle-nosed whale |
| *Ziphius cavirostris* | Cuvier's whale |
| *Mesoplodon bidens* | Sowerby's whale |
| **Family** Monodontidae | |
| *Delphinapterus leucas* | white whale |
| *Monodon monoceros* | narwhal |
| **Family** Phocoenidae | porpoises |
| *Phocoena phocoena* | harbour porpoise |
| **Family** Delphinidae | dolphins |
| *Orcinus orca* | killer whale |
| *Globicephala melaena* | long-finned pilot whale |
| *Grampus griseus* | Risso's dolphin |
| *Lagenorhynchus albirostris* | white-beaked dolphin |
| *Lagenorhynchus acutus* | white-sided dolphin |
| *Tursiops truncatus* | bottle-nosed dolphin |
| *Stenella coeruteoalba* | Euphrosyne dolphin |
| *Delphinus delphis* | common dolphin |
| | |
| **Order** Carnivora | carnivores |
| **Family** Canidae | dogs |
| *Vulpes vulpes* | fox |
| **Family** Mustelidae | |
| *Martes martes* | pine marten |
| *Mustela erminea* | stoat |
| *Mustela nivalis* | weasel |
| *Mustela putorius* | polecat |
| *Mustela furo* | ferret |
| *Mustela vison* | mink |
| *Meles meles* | badger |
| *Lutra lutra* | otter |
| **Family** Felidae | cats |
| *Felis silvestris* | wild cat |
| | |
| **Order** Pinnipedia | pinnipedes |
| **Family** Phocidae | seals |
| *Phoca vitulina* | common seal |
| *Halichoerus grypus* | grey seal |
| *Phoca hispida* | ringed seal |
| *Pagophilus groenlandicus* | harp seal |
| *Erignathus barbatus* | bearded seal |
| *Cystophora cristata* | hooded seal |
| | |
| **Order** Perissodactyla | odd-toed ungulates |
| **Family** Equidae | horses |
| Equus | horse |
| | |
| **Order** Artiodactyla | even-toed ungulates |
| **Family** Cervidae | deer |
| *Cervus elaphus* | red deer |

| | |
|---|---|
| *Cervus nippon* | sika deer |
| *Dama dama* | fallow deer |
| *Capreolus capreolus* | roe deer |
| *Muntiacus reevesi* | muntjac |
| *Hydropotes inermis* | water deer |
| *Rangifer tarandus* | reindeer |
| **Family** Bovidae | |
| *Bos* | wild cattle |
| *Capra* | feral goat |
| *Ovis* | feral sheep |

# Appendix II Mammals and the law

At the time of writing there is not a good published summary of British legislation affecting mammals, but J. F. D. Frazer has produced a very good paper on this theme which was circulated to Mammal Society members in 1980 with their Newsletter 42. I hope that this will be produced in a final version as a Society publication shortly.

Of the Acts and Conventions concerning mammals to date, the Deer Act 1963, Conservation of Seals Act 1970, Badgers Act 1973 and the International Whaling Conventions are probably of the greatest interest to the mammal watcher.

Although only two rare bats (mouse-eared and greater horseshoe) were included in the Conservation of Wild Creatures and Wild Plants Act, 1975, bat banding may only take place under licence from the Nature Conservancy and I urge all watchers who want to handle by capture any type of mammal or disturb wildlife in any way during watching to treat their subjects with the respect and care they deserve.

The important Wildlife and Countryside Bill is in preparation as this book goes to press. I hope this bill has successful progress through both Houses of Parliament.

# Appendix III Useful addresses

**G. Andrews Engineering,** Pound Green, Upper Arley, Bewdley, Worcs DY12 3LE. Suppliers of several types of Arley metal high seats which are safe and well constructed.

**J. Barbour & Son Ltd.,** Simonside, South Shields, Tyne and Wear NE34 9PD. Suppliers of all-weather drab coloured outdoor clothing. The Solway zipper coat is warm, waterproof and merges with cover. (*See also* **J. Norris of Penrith** and **Hebden Cord Co. Ltd.**)

**Dr Peter Beamish,** Village Inn, Trinity Bay, Newfoundland, Canada. Organises whale watching trips and holidays. (*See also* **Friends of the Earth** and **Greenpeace.**)

**Biological Records Centre** *see* **Institute of Terrestrial Ecology**

**The British Deer Society,** The Mill House, Bishopstrow, Warminster, Wilts BA12 9HJ.

**British Naturalists' Association,** 43 Warnford Road, Tilehurst, Reading, Berks. Libraries will give the address of the local branch secretary. One of the best ways of getting to know the countryside around your home is to join this association which has branch membership and organised rambles. Friendly and non-specialist. Publish *Country-side* magazine.

**British Trust for Ornithology,** Beech Grove, Tring, Herts. Suppliers of Pesola scales for weighing mammals.

**Cats' Accessories Ltd.,** Catac House, 1 Newnham Street, Bedford MK40 3JR. Suppliers of small feeder bottles and teats for rearing wild mammals rescued when very young.

**Cetacean Group,** c/o Dr P. Evans, Mammal Society, Edward Grey Institute, Department of Zoology, South Parks Road, Oxford OX1 3PS. Supply information on whale distribution and cetacean survey record sheets. All whale sightings in British waters should be reported to them.

**C.T.F. Ltd.,** 11 Langley Park Road, Sutton, Surrey. Suppliers of decoy calls and ferreting equipment.

**The Fauna & Flora Preservation Society,** Honorary Secretary, D. M. Jones, c/o Zoological Society of London, Regent's Park, London NW1 4RY.

**Ferret Society,** c/o G. Wellstead, Secretary, Ormsby, Kingsway Avenue, Woking, Surrey.

**Friends of the Earth,** 9 Poland Street, London W1. Undertake many conservation projects connected with mammal ecology.

**Gilbertson & Page,** Corry's Roestock Lane, Colney Heath, St. Albans, Herts AL4 0QW. Publish *Gamekeeper and Countryside* magazine. Suppliers of various products including Renardine mammal repellent.

**Greenpeace,** Colombo Street, London SE1. Undertake whale and seal conservation projects.

**Hebden Cord Co. Ltd.,** 17 Oldgate, Hebden Bridge, West Yorkshire HX7 6EW. Suppliers of country clothing, plus-four type trousers including 'moleskins'.

**Nicholas Hunter Ltd.,** 16B Worcester Place, Oxford. Suppliers of storage systems for colour slides of all types.

**Institute of Terrestrial Ecology,** Monks Wood Experimental Station, Abbots Ripton, Huntingdon PE17 2LS. Contact Dr R. E. Stebbings for help with bat problems.

**Kings,** PO Box 17, Dorking, Surrey RH4 2PQ. Lamping (Quartz Halogen bulb) outfits for watching with binoculars at night.

**Longworth Scientific Instruments,** Radley Road, Abingdon, Berks. Suppliers of Longworth box traps for small mammals.

**The Mammal Conservation Trust Ltd.,** c/o Dr Oliver Dansie, Bridge Cottage, Welwyn, Herts. Undertakes all types of mammal management and conservation projects.

**The Mammal Society,** Harvest House, 62 London Road, Reading, Berks RG1 5AS. An advisory body which will give information and advice on all mammal questions. Many booklet publications can be obtained from them; *see also* Further reading. Open to all interested in mammal study.

**National Geographic Society,** 17th & M Street NW, Washington DC, USA 20036. Supply whale charts and other excellent material on mammals published in association with their magazine.

**Nature Conservancy Council,** Calthorpe House, Calthorpe Street, Banbury, Oxford *and* Ffordd Penrhos, Bangor, Gwynedd, Wales *and* 12 Hope Terrace, Edinburgh, Scotland.

**John Norris of Penrith,** Dept. S.T., 21 Victoria Road, Penrith, Cumbria CA11 8HP. Suppliers of competitively priced country clothing of all kinds including Uniroyal Hunter boots.

**Opticron,** Unit 6, 25 Lattimore Road, Marlborough Trading Estate, St. Albans, Herts. Suppliers of binoculars and telescopes with opportunity to try out types overlooking extensive views.

**Otter Trust,** Earsham, Nr Bungay, Suffolk.

**Q.M.C. Instruments Ltd.,** 229 Mile End Road, London E1 4AA. Supply bat detectors including the mini bat detector.

**Royal Society for the Protection of Birds,** The Lodge, Sandy, Beds SG19 2DL. Sell many good publications which also relate to mammals including: *Nature Photographer's Code of Practice.* Their well-managed reserves help protect the habitat for mammals also, for example, otters in wetland reserves.

**Society for the Promotion of Nature Conservation,** The Green, Nettleham, Lincoln LN2 2NR. This is the parent body of the local Naturalists' Trusts and has nature reserves managed by the local branches throughout Britain. Libraries will give the address of the local secretary. Also publish a *Focus on Bats* leaflet for help with bat problems.

**Edward Stamford Ltd.,** 12–14 Longacre, London WC2E 9LP. Stock a wide variety of maps from all countries; also operate a mail order service.

**Synthetic Fabrics (Scotland) Ltd.,** Low and Bonar Textiles Division, Victoria Works, Forfar, Angus DD8 3BS Scotland. Suppliers of material for hides: hessian in durable tan polypropylene.

**Wildlife Publications Ltd.,** 100 Great Portland Street, London W1N 3PD. Publish *Wildlife*, a monthly magazine which has a high standard of mammal photography.

**The World Wildlife Fund UK,** Panda House, 29 Greville Street, London EC1N 8AX. Represented in 26 countries to raise money for conservation projects throughout the world. Particularly concerned with threatened species and habitats.

**Young's of Misterton,** Crewkerne, Somerset. Suppliers of decoys and squeak calls and lures for mammals such as 'Draw Game' and 'Fox Lure'. Aniseed based, these preparations can be useful, for example, to attract badgers into culverts when diverted from new roads.

# Further reading

The following books and a few papers are selected to give about a hundred useful references. All make good further reading or cover particular aspects of mammal study referred to in the preparation of this book. I have not listed all the many scientific papers published which have built up my own knowledge of mammals, but Corbet and Southern's (eds.) *Handbook of British Mammals* (1977) and Walker's *Mammals of the World* (1975) have extensive bibliographies and Chapman compiled a detailed deer bibliography in Dansie and Wince's *Deer of the World* (1968–70).

Angel, H. *Nature Photography*. Fountain Press, 1972.

Bang, P. and Dahlstrom, P. *Animal tracks and signs*. Collins, 1974.

Banks, C., Clark, M. and Newton, R. *Observations on an unusual mixed roost of Serotine and Noctule Bats in East Hertfordshire*. Trans. Herts Nat. His. Soc. 28:3, 20–22, 1980.

Barret-Hamilton, G. E. H. and Hinton, M. A. C. *A History of British Mammals*. Gurney & Jackson, 1910–21.

Beard, P. H. *The End of the Game*. Hamlyn, 1965.

Bonner, W. N. *Whales*. Blandford Press, 1980.

Brink, F. H. van den. *A field guide to the mammals of Britain and Europe*. Collins, 1967.

Brower, K. *Wake of the Whale*. (With photographs by William R. Curtsinger.) Friends of the Earth, 1979.

Brown, J. and Stoddart, D. *Killing mammals and general post-mortem methods*. Mammal Rev. 7:2, Chapter 7. Mammal Society/Blackwell, 1977.

Burrows, R. *Wild Fox*. David & Charles, 1968.

Burton, M. *The Hedgehog*. André Deutsch, 1969.

Cadman, A. *Dawn, Dusk and Deer*. Country Life Books, 1966.

Calhoun, J. B. *The ecology and sociology of the Norway Rat*. US Dept. Health, Education and Welfare, 1962.

Carrington, R. and Matthews, L. H. (eds.) *The Living World of Animals*. Reader's Digest Association, 1970.

Chapman, N. and Chapman, D. *Fallow Deer*. British Deer Society, 1970.

Chapman, D. I. and Chapman, N. G. *Fallow Deer: their history distribution and biology*. Terence Dalton, 1975.

Clark, M. Fraying by muntjac. *Deer* 1, 272–3, 1968.
*The Conservation of Badgers in Hertfordshire*. Trans. Herts. Nat. Hist. Soc. 27:2, 39–47, 1970.
*The Survey of Mammals, Reptiles and Amphibia in Hertfordshire (Annual Reports)*. Trans. Herts. Nat. Hist. Soc, 1970–80.

Clark, M. and Summers, S. *Seasonal Population Movements of Brown Rats and House Mice in East Hertfordshire*. Trans. Herts. Nat. Hist. Soc. 28:3, 17–19, 1980.

Corbet, G. B. *The terrestrial mammals of Western Europe*. Foulis and Co., 1966.
Provisional distribution maps of British mammals. Mammal Rev. 1, 95–142. Mammal Society/Blackwell, 1971.
*The mammals of the Palaearctic Region: a taxonomic review*. British Museum (Nat. His.), 1978.

Corbet, G. B. and Southern, H. N. (eds.) *The Handbook of British Mammals.* Mammal Society/Blackwell, 1977.

Cott, H. *Looking at Animals.* Collins, 1975.

Cowan, D. *The Wild Rabbit.* Mammal Society/Blandford Press, 1980.

Croin Michielson, N. Intraspecific and interspecific competition in the shrews *Sorex araneus* L. and *Sorex minutus* L. Bull. Mammal Soc. 28, 6–7, 1967.

Crowcroft, W. P. *The Life of the Shrew.* Max Reinhardt, 1957.

Dansie, O. *Muntjac.* British Deer Society, 1970.

Dansie, O. and Wince, W. *Deer of the World.* East Anglian Branch of the British Deer Society, 1968–70.

Davies, B. and Porter, E. *Seal Song.* Allen Lane, 1978.

Evans, H. *Pictures on a Page.* Heinemann, 1978.

Evans, P. G. H. *An analysis of sightings of Cetacea in British waters.* Mammal Rev. 6, 5–14. Mammal Society/Blackwell, 1975.
  *Cetaceans in British Waters.* Mammal Rev. 10:1, 1–52. Mammal Society/Blackwell, 1980.

Ewer, R. F. *The Carnivores.* Weidenfeld & Nicolson, 1973.

Fairley, J. S. *An Irish Beast Book.* Blackstaff Press, 1975.

Glue, D. E. *Prey taken by the Barn Owl in England and Wales.* Bird Study 14, 169–83, 1967.
  *Food of the barn owl in Britain and Ireland.* Bird Study 21, 200–10, 1974.

Godfrey, G. K. and Crowcroft, P. *The Life of the Mole.* Museum Press, 1960.

Gotch, A. F. *Mammals – Their Latin Names Explained.* Blandford Press, 1979.

Grzimek, B. *Animal Life Encyclopedia Mammals.* Vols. 10–13. Van Nostrand Reinhold, 1972.

Harris, C. J. *Otters: a study of the recent Lutrinae.* Weidenfeld & Nicolson, 1968.

Harris, R. A. and Duff, K. R. *Wild Deer in Britain.* David & Charles, 1970.

Harris, S. *Secret Life of the Harvest Mouse.* Hamlyn, 1979.
  *The Harvest Mouse.* Blandford Press, 1980.

Hawker, J. *A Victorian Poacher: James Hawker's Journal.* Oxford University Press, 1961.

Herter, K. *Hedgehogs.* Phoenix House, 1965.

Hewer, H. R. *British Seals.* Collins, 1974.

Hooper, J. H. D. Use of the Holgate Ultrasonic Receiver to obtain bat distribution data in the Thames Valley and adjacent areas to the west of London. The Middle-Thames Naturalist: 29, 4–13, 1976.

Horwood, M. T. and Masters, E. H. *Sika Deer.* British Deer Society, 1970.

Hurrell, E. *Dormice.* Animals of Britain No. 10, Sunday Times Publications, 1962.
  *Watch for the Otter.* Country Life Books, 1963.
  *The Common Dormouse* Mammal Society/Blandford Press, 1980.

Hurrell, H. G. *Pine Martens.* Animals of Britain No. 22, Sunday Times Publications, 1963.

Jefferies, R. *The Gamekeeper at Home.* John Murray, 1914.

King, J. E. *Seals of the World.* British Museum (Nat. His.), 1964.

Lawrence, M. J. and Brown, R. W. *Mammals of Britain, their tracks, trails and Signs.* Blandford Press, 1973.

Lever, C. *The Naturalized Animals of the British Isles.* Hutchinson, 1977.
Linn, I. *Weasels.* Animals of Britain No. 14, Sunday Times Publications, 1962.
Lockley, R. M. *The Private Life of the Rabbit.* André Deutsch, 1965.
*Whales, Dolphins and Porpoises.* David & Charles, 1979.
*Grey Seal, Common Seal.* André Deutsch, 1966.
Lorenz, K. *King Solomon's Ring.* Methuen, 1952.
*Man meets Dog.* Methuen, 1954.
Lydekker, R. *The deer of all Lands.* Rowland Ward, 1898.
McNally, L. *Year of the Red Deer.* Dent, 1975.
Matheson, C. *Brown Rats.* Animals of Britain No. 16, Sunday Times Publications, 1962.
Matthews, L. H. *British Mammals.* Collins, 1952.
Mellanby, K. *The Mole.* Collins, 1971.
Millais, J. G. *The Mammals of Great Britain and Ireland.* Vols I–III. Longman, 1905.
Neal, E. G. *The Badger.* Collins, 1948. (Also Pelican Books, 1958.)
*Otters.* Animals of Britain No. 8, Sunday Times Publications, 1962.
*National Badger Survey.* Mammal Rev. 2, 55–64. Mammal Society/Blackwell, 1972.
*Badgers.* Blandford Press, 1977.
Novick, A. *The World of Bats.* (With photographs by Nina Leen.) Holt, Rinehart & Winston, 1969.
Page, F. J. T. (ed.) *Field Guide to British Deer.* Blackwell, 2nd ed., 1971.
Prior, R. *Roe Stalking.* Percival Marshall, 1963.
*The Roe Deer of Cranborne Chase: an ecological survey.* Oxford University Press, 1968.
Ransome, R. *The Greater Horseshoe Bat.* Mammal Society/Blandford Press, 1980.
Roberts, T. *The Mammals of Pakistan.* Ernest Benn, 1977.
Ryder, S. R. *Water Voles.* Animals of Britain No. 4, Sunday Times Publications, 1962.
Shorten, M. *Squirrels.* Collins, 1954.
*Grey Squirrels.* Animals of Britain No. 5, Sunday Times Publications, 1962.
*Red Squirrels.* Animals of Britain No. 6, Sunday Times Publications, 1962.
Soper, E. A. *When Badgers Wake.* Routledge & Kegan Paul, 1955.
*Muntjac.* Longman, 1969.
Soper, T. *The Bird Table Book.* Macdonald/David & Charles, 1965.
Spradbery, J. *Wasps.* Sidgwick & Jackson, 1973.
Staines, B. *The Red Deer.* Mammal Society/Blandford Press, 1980.
Stebbings, R. E. *A bat new to Britain Pipistrellus nathusii with notes on its identification and distribution in Europe.* J. Zool. London 161, 282–6, 1970.
*Artificial roosts for bats.* J. Devon Trust Nat. Conserv. 6, 114–19, 1974.
Stephen, D. *Watching Wildlife.* Collins, 1963.
Thompson, H. V. and Worden, A. *The Rabbit.* Collins, 1956.
Tittensor, A. *The Red Squirrel.* Mammal Society/Blandford Press, 1980.

Twigg, G. *The Brown Rat*. David & Charles, 1975.
*Techniques with captive mammals*. Mammal Rev. 7:2 Chapter 6. Mammal Society/Blackwell, 1977.
Walker, E. P. *Mammals of the World*, 3 vols. (3rd edn.) Johns Hopkins Press, 1975.
Walton, K. C. *The distribution of the polecat. (Putorius putorius) in England, Wales and Scotland, 1959–62*. Proc. Zool. Soc. Lond. 143, 333–6, 1964.
*The distribution of the polecat. (Putorius putorius) in Great Britain, 1963–67*. J. Zool. Soc. Lond. 155, 237–40, 1968.
Warner, L. J. *Mammal Photography and Observation*. Academic Press, 1978.
Wayre, P. *The Private Life of the Otter*. Batsford, 1979.
Webb, Jean *Otter spraint analysis*. Mammal Society, Reading.
Whitehead, G. K. *The Deer of Great Britain and Ireland: an account of their history, status and distribution*. Routledge & Kegan Paul, 1964.
*The Wild Goats of Great Britain and Ireland*. David & Charles, 1972.
*Deer of the World*. Constable, 1972.
Wimsatt, W. A. *Biology of Bats*. (3 vols.) Academic Press, 1970 & 1977.
Yalden, D. W. *Identification of remains in owl pellets*. Mammal Society, Reading, 1977.
Yalden, D. W. Morris, P. A. *The Lives of Bats*. David & Charles, 1975.

# Acknowledgements

## Colour photographs

Ardea: Ian Beames 108 bottom, Anthony and Elizabeth Bomford 105 top, 125 bottom, François Gohier 144; C. Banks 90 bottom; Michael Clark 17 top, 18 top, 35 top and bottom, 72 top, 89 top and bottom, 90 top, 107 bottom; Bruce Coleman: S. C. Bisserot 36, 53 top and bottom, 54 top and bottom, Jane Burton 71, Hans Reinhard 108 top; Geoffrey Kinns 18 bottom, Nature Photographers: Owen Newman 17 bottom, 72 bottom; Ralph Newton 34 bottom, 126 top and bottom; Oxford Scientific Films: G. I. Bernard 125 top, Marty Stouffer/Animals Animals 143.

## Black-and-white photographs

Aquila: A. Faulkner-Taylor 114 top, H. A. Hems 121, W. S. Paton 141 top and bottom, M. C. Wilkes 79; Ardea: I. and L. Beames 38, Werner Curth 65, François Gohier 136, P. Morris 111, Serge and Dominique Simon 74, Robert T. Smith 69; C. Banks 76; Michael Clark 9, 14 top and bottom, 26, 27, 28, 29, 34, 55, 61, 62 bottom, 67 top and bottom, 85 top and bottom, 86 top, 87 bottom, 88, 93, 102, 104, 114 bottom, 118, 128, 131, 147, 152, 158, 161; Peter Delap 87 top; Eric Hosking 77, 110, 117; Ben Gaskell 66; Geoffrey Kinns 41, 42, 45, 46, 83, 112, 130, 133, 140 top, Tom Kittle 62 top; Peter Loughran 78; Ralph Newton 48, 63; Ralph and Neil Newton 60

# Index

Page references in italic refer to illustrations.

Badger, 13, 21, 27, 28, 29, 70, 120, 122, 123–9, *126*: cubs, 124, *126*, *128*; drawing, 160; field signs, 129; Ministry of Agriculture F.F. research, 13; photography, 127, 128; on tape, 158–9; tuberculosis in, 163; watching, *14*, 15, 20, 46, 84, 123–9, *123*
*Barbastella barbastellus*, 59
Bats, 21, 27, 28, 29, 50–68: barbastelle, 56, 58; Bechstein's, *53*, 56, *58*; boxes, 68, *68*; Brandt's, *58*; capture, 50–6, 62; caves and ice houses, 65–6, *66*, *67*; Daubenton's, 56, *58*, 62–4, *63*, 65; detector, 55–6, 55; echolocation, 52, 55–6, 66; European free-tailed, 6; greater horseshoe, *36*, 56, *58*, 65, 66, *66*, 76; grey long-eared, 56; hibernation, 65; Leisler's, *54*, 56, *58*; lesser horseshoe, 56, *58*, 65, 76; long-eared, 56, *58*, 64–5, *65*; measurement, 62, *149*; mouse-eared, 56, *58*; Nathusius' pipistrelle, 55, *58*; natterer's, *53*, 56, *58*, 64, *67*, 76; net, *51*, 55; noctule, 56, *58*, 59–62, *62*, *63*; pipistrelle, 50, *54*, 56, *58*, 62, 63, 64, *67*; recognition details, 57–9; serotine, 56, *58*, 59–62, *60*, *61*; silhouettes, *58*; whiskered, 56, *58*, 64
Beech marten, 116
Binoculars, 12–15, 20, 59, 61, 77, 79, 92, 94, 116, 120, 121, 127; night, *14*, 121, 127
Biological Records Centre, 142
British Deer Society, 86
British Trust for Ornithology, 148

Camouflage, of watcher, 8, *9*, 15
*Capra hircus* 6
Carnivores, 118, *see also* Predators
Cetaceans, 134–8; propulsion, *136*; *see also* Whales
Chamois, 6, 27

Chinese water deer, 70, 84, *90*, 92, 98, 101, 102, 106–110: barking, *90*, 109; fawns *90*, 106; feeding 102–3, 109; fighting, 101; late oestrous, 84; rut, 109; Whipsnade, 106, 109; Woburn, 106
Clothing, 10–12
County trusts, 115, 145
Coypu, 29, 80, *80*

Deer, 21, 25, 27, 29, 81, 83–110, 122: antlers, 83–4; barking, 84; catch-ups, 84–6, *85*, *86*, 120; fraying, 84; hand-reared, 93, 104–5; rut, 84; scrape, 84; terminology, 84; territory, 84; velvet, *83*, 84; wallow, 84; watching techniques, 84
Deer Society, 145
Diary, 20, 59–60, 113, *147*, *147*
Dolphins, 29, 134–7, *136*: bottle-nosed, *135*, 136; common, *135*, 136, *136*, *144*; euphrosyne, *135*, 137; Risso's, *135*, 137; white-beaked, *135*, 136; white-sided, *135*, 136; *see also* Whales
Drawing, 150, 159–63; equipment, 160–3, *161*; scraperboard, *162*

*Eliomys quercinus*, 6
*Eptesicus serotinus*, 57

Fallow deer, 28, *72*, 92–4: fawn, *93*; menil colour, 92; rut, 93; watching, 92–4
Fauna and Flora Preservation Society, 145
Ferret, 31: detector, 118; polecat and, 116–9, *118*; Society, 119, 168; working, 118
Fox, 21, 25, 26, 27, 28, 29, 70, 116, 119–23, 163: baiting, 120, 122; barking, 120; cubs, 19, 121–2, *121*, 125; and chickens, 123; diet and feeding, 120–1, *125*; hunting, 119; lure, 120;

and muntjac, 122; screams, 120; watching, 14, 120–2

Garden dormouse, 6
Goat, 29: feral and sheep, 111–2; rut, 112
Grey squirrel, 76, 78, *78*, 79
*Gytropus*, 66

Habitats, 21, 24–9: fir plantations, 29; Forestry Commission, 21; gardens, 27; moorland and mountain, 29; old deciduous woodland, 28; old pits, gravel workings and refuse tips, 29, *29*; open farmland and estates, 27; parks, open spaces and golf courses, 27; rivers, estuaries and the coast, 29; wetland, marshes, ponds and lakes, 29, *29*
Hare, brown, 27, 28, *71*, 73–5, *73*, *74*, 76: courtship, *74*, 75; mountain, 75–6, *76*; population, 73
Hedgehog, 27, 28, *35*, 47–9: defence, *48*; nest, *18*; swimming, *48*
Hides, 21–4, *22*, *23*, 84
High seats, 21, 24, *24*, 79; Arley, *24*, 84
Horse, 82–3: breeds, 82; Carmargue, 82; Exmoor, 82; home range, 82–3; pony, 29; territory, 82–3

Ibex, 6, 111

Kangaroo, 81

Longworth trap, 6, 34, *34*, 37

Mammal, classification of, 164–7; and the law, 167; hunting, 163
Mammal Society, 132, 134, 142,

145; trap loan scheme, 37
Mammal table, 27, *30*
Manuscripts, preparation of, 148
Marine mammals, 134–41
Marsupial, 81
Millais, J.G., 50, 52, 133
Mink, 29; otters and, 129–32: watching, 132; water voles and, 132
Mole, 38–9, *38*, 142
Molossidae, 6
Mouse, 21, 25, 43–7, 69: common dormouse, *17*, 28, 46–7, *47*, nest, *44*, 76; edible dormouse, 31, 45, *46*, enclosure, *32*; harvest, 8, 28, 33, *33*, 43, *47*; house, 30, *33*, 34, 44; nest, 18, *44*, nest site, *28*; photography, *154*; points of identification, *33*; wood, *17*, 30, 31–3, *33*, 43, 76, 121: yellow-necked, 30, 32, *33*, 34, 43
Muntjac, 20, 22, 28, 84, *89*, 95–106: activity routines, 96, *100*; antlers, 101, 102, *102*, *103*; barking, 97–8, *97*, *98*; catch-up, 84–6, *85*, *86*; clicking, 97; collars, 85, *86*, defence of fawns, 122; fawns, 104–6, *104*, *105*; feeding, 102; fighting, 99–101, *100*; and fox, 122; fraying, 99, *100*; habitats, 96; hand-rearing, 102, 104–5, *104*; oestrous, 97, 102; scent, 101; scraping, 99; sounds and displays, 96–7; stamping, 98; territory, 98–101; tracks, *99*; watching, 95
*Myotis*, 56, 57, 59, 65; *bechsteini*, 57; *brandti*, 57; *daubentoni*, 57; *myotis*, 57; *mystacinus*, 57; *nattereri*, 57

Natural History Societies, 142, 148
Notebook, 20, 147
*Nyctalus leisleri*, 57; *noctula*, 57

Ordnance survey maps, 145, *146*
Otter, 25, 29, *130*, 143, 163:

couches, 131; food, 130; holts, 132; hunts, 129–30, and mink, 129–32; resting sites, 131; spraint, *131*; watching, 131
Owl pellet analysis, 25, *25*

Photography, 150–7: badger, 127, 128; choice of equipment and film, 151–5, *152*; deer, 86; film making, *154*; flash, 154–5, *154*, 159; macro, 153, 154; projectors, 156–7; publishing, 156
Pine marten, *29*, *108*, 115–6: in captivity, 116; pathways, 116
*Plecotus auritus* 59; *austriacus*, 59
*Pipistrellus pipistrellus*, *54*, 59, 67, *nathusii*, 59
Polecat, 29, 31, 40, *108*: in captivity, 116, 118; and ferret, 116–9, *118*, 132; hair colour, 117–8
Porpoises, 29, 134–7: harbour, *135*, 136; *see also* Whales
Predators, 113–33: conservation of, 115; hunting by, 115

Rabbits, 21, 25, 26, 27, 28, 29, 69–73, *69*: aggression, 70; and badgers, 129, courtship, 70; display, 69; management, 118–9; myxomatosis, 70; warrens and ferrets, 118
Rat, black, 44, *45*; brown, 29, 31, 44, 45, 101, damage by, 44–5, 69; with stoat, *114*
Records, 142–9: grid references, 145–8, *146*; measurements and equipment for, 148–9, *149*; skins, 149
Red deer, 22–3, 29, 76, 86–91, *87*: calving, 91; hinds, 88, 91; rut, *87*, *88*, 91; stags, 87, *88*; stalking, 86
Red-necked wallaby, 81–2, *81*
Red squirrel, 76–8, *77*, 116
Reed warbler, nest, *44*
Reindeer, 92, 110, *110*
Rhinolophidae, 57
Roe deer, 28, 76, 94–5: antlers,

94; calls and lures, 94–5; fawns, 94; photography, 95; rut, 95; watching, 94
Royal Society for the Protection of Birds, 13
*Rupicapra rupicapra*, 6

Seals, 23, 29, 110: common and grey, 139–41, *140*; bearded, 139; breeding, 139–41, *141*; Farne Islands, 110, 139, 140; harp, 139; hooded, 139; pup, *141*; ringed, 139; territories, 140–1
Sheep, feral goats and, 111–2; Soay, 112, *112*
Shrew, 31, 39, 43: common, *33*, 39, 40, 76; pygmy, *33*, 35, 39, 76; water, 29, *33*, 40; white-toothed, *33*, 40
Sika deer, 72, 91–2: antlers, 92; calving, 92; field signs, 91; flamel, 92; Formosan, 92; Japanese, 92; Manchurian, 92; New Forest, 91; rut, 91, 92; territory, 92
Slides, storage and classification of, 157
Small mammals, 30–49
*Sorex araneus*, 164; *minutus*, 164
Sound recording, 92, 150, 157–9, *158*; choice of equipment, 157–8; microphone and parabola, 158–9, *158*
Stalking, 8–9, 15, 16–19
Stoat, 21, 27, 28, 29, 76, *107*, *114*, 116: and weasels, 113–5; measurement, *149*; photography, 151–2; predation on rabbit, 113, 119
Swept path, *26*

*Tadarida teniotis*, 6
Talks, 156–7
Tarpan, 82
Telescope, 15, 87
Tracks, 87

Vespertilionidae, 57

Vole, 25, 41–3, 44, 114, 120:
  bank, 30, 31, *33*, 41, 42, 121;
  field, 30, *33*, 41, 42, 43, 121;
  and mink, 132; Orkney, 42;
  runs and nests, *41*; water, 23,
  29, 42–3, *42*

**W**apiti, 88
Weasel, 27, 28, 29, *107*: and
  badger, 129; captive, 114;
  hunting, 115; stoats and, 113–
  5, *114*, 119; watching, 115
Whales, 29, 134–8, *135*, *136*, 163:
  beaked spp., *135*, 137; blue,
  *138*; bowhead, 138; Bryde's,
  *138*; fin, *135*, *136*, 137, *138*;
  grey, 136, *138*; humpback,
  *135*, 136, 137, *138*; minke, *135*,
  137, 138; narwhal, *135*, 137;
  northern bottlenose, *135*, 137;
  pygmy sperm, *135*, 137; right,
  *135*, 137, *138*; sei, *135*, 137,
  *138*; sightings in British
  waters, 135; sperm, *135*, 137,
  *138*; wallcharts, 136; whaling,
  136; white, *135*, 137
White cattle, 110–11, *111*
Wild cat, 29, 132–3, *133*: domestic, 10; interbreeding with
  domestic, 132–3